Flipped Learning in Physical Education

This is the first book to introduce flipped learning in the context of physical education. It is a timely exploration of pedagogical approaches that draw on digital technologies that can allow learning online and at a distance to support important learning time for physical activity.

The book discusses the role of online and digital technology in education, and physical education more specifically, and examines the key features that define flipped learning, its boundaries, and its format. Drawing on modern learning theories, the book explains why educators and practitioners may choose to use flipped learning and how the approach can improve physical activity opportunities. It also considers the challenges and the guiding principles involved in implementing flipped learning in different countries, cultures, and contexts.

Full of practical guidance, and drawing on cutting-edge research, this book is invaluable reading for all students, researchers, pre-service and in-service teachers, and coaches working in physical education or youth sport.

Ove Østerlie is an associate professor in physical education in the Department of Art, Physical Education and Sports at the Norwegian University of Science and Technology, Norway, where he teaches and researches physical education. His research is focused on the implementation of digital tools in physical education and research on students with concentration difficulties.

Chad Killian is an assistant professor in the Department of Kinesiology at the University of New Hampshire, USA. His primary interests relate to studying the use and efficacy of digital instruction in physical education. He seeks to understand the extent to which technology-based approaches to teaching and learning can expand quality physical education and promote positive outcomes in physical education environments.

Julia Sargent is a lecturer at the Institute of Educational Technology at the Open University, UK. Her work focuses on the use of technologies for teaching and learning, the exploration of physical education, and pedagogy in higher education.

Routledge Focus on Sport Pedagogy

Series editor: Ash Casey
Loughborough University, UK

The field of sport pedagogy (physical education and coaching) is united by the desire to improve the experiences of young people and adult participants. The *Routledge Focus on Sport Pedagogy* series presents small books on big topics in an effort to eradicate the boundaries that currently exist between young people, adult learners, coaches, teachers and academics, in schools, clubs, and universities. Theoretically grounded but with a strong emphasis on practice, the series aims to open up important and useful new perspectives on teaching, coaching, and learning in sport and physical education.

Meaningful Physical Education
An Approach for Teaching and Learning
Edited by Tim Fletcher, Déirdre Ní Chróinín, Douglas Gleddie and Stephanie Beni

Pedagogies of Social Justice in Physical Education and Youth Sport
Shrehan Lynch, Jennifer L. Walton-Fisette and Carla Luguetti

Learner-Oriented Teaching and Assessment in Youth Sport
Edited by Cláudio Farias and Isabel Mesquita

Physical Education Pedagogies for Health
Edited by Lorraine Cale and Jo Harris

Flipped Learning in Physical Education
Opportunities and Applications
Ove Østerlie, Chad Killian and Julia Sargent

For more information about this series, please visit: https://www.routledge.com/Routledge-Focus-on-Sport-Pedagogy/book-series/RFSPED

Flipped Learning in Physical Education

Opportunities and Applications

Ove Østerlie, Chad Killian, and Julia Sargent

Routledge
Taylor & Francis Group

LONDON AND NEW YORK

First published 2023
by Routledge
4 Park Square, Milton Park, Abingdon, Oxon OX14 4RN

and by Routledge
605 Third Avenue, New York, NY 10158

Routledge is an imprint of the Taylor & Francis Group, an informa business

© 2023 Ove Østerlie, Chad Killian and Julia Sargent

The right of Ove Østerlie, Chad Killian and Julia Sargent to be identified as authors of this work has been asserted in accordance with sections 77 and 78 of the Copyright, Designs and Patents Act 1988.

British Library Cataloguing-in-Publication Data
A catalogue record for this book is available from the British Library

Library of Congress Cataloging-in-Publication Data
Names: Østerlie, Ove, author. | Killian, Chad, author. | Sargent, Julia, author.
Title: Flipped learning in physical education : opportunities and applications / Ove Østerlie, Chad Killian and Julia Sargent.
Description: Abingdon, Oxon ; New York City : Routledge, 2023. | Series: Routledge focus on sport pedagogy | Includes bibliographical references and index.
Identifiers: LCCN 2022022974 | ISBN 9781032036717 (hardback) | ISBN 9781032066844 (paperback) | ISBN 9781003203377 (ebook)
Subjects: LCSH: Physical education and training--Web-based instruction. | Flipped classrooms. | Blended learning.
Classification: LCC GV364 .O77 2023 | DDC 796.071--dc23/eng/20220624
LC record available at https://lccn.loc.gov/2022022974

ISBN: 978-1-032-03671-7 (hbk)
ISBN: 978-1-032-06684-4 (pbk)
ISBN: 978-1-003-20337-7 (ebk)

DOI: 10.4324/9781003203377

Typeset in Times New Roman
by MPS Limited, Dehradun

Ove – to my family who inspires me to explore, stay positive, work hard, and live life.

Chad – to Lauren, my wife and partner in scholarship.

Julia – to my mum, a retired PE teacher.

Contents

Figures

Tables

Acknowledgements

To all the teachers, students, schools, and academics who have challenged and developed our thinking of flipped learning in physical education. We appreciate having had the opportunity to work alongside all of you, in workshops, present and online classes, through chats in hallways, and in more formal settings. We believe both the community of physical education and the ever-growing community of flipped learning promoters and practitioners must come together even more to thrive and for the field to expand, develop, and give fruitful contributions to student learning and teacher experiences.

1 Introduction to Flipped Learning in Physical Education

Introduction and rationale behind the book

This book covers the topic of flipped learning (FL) in physical education (PE). Each of the authors has both personal and professional interest in not only the subject of PE but also the use of FL within it. Having conducted research within this topic area, we were struck by the lack of consensus and research available to us and others. We were acutely aware that FL is a relatively under-researched area of PE (Daum & Buschner, 2014, 2018; Killian et al., 2019; Sargent & Casey, 2020). That being said, we knew that there was increasing evidence to suggest that FL creates potential for areas such as physical activity, and practice opportunities such as extra instructional feedback (Killian et al., 2016). The strengths of this approach for the subject of PE we felt were important to explore in this book given the often-restricted curriculum time for PE (Castelli & Rink, 2003) and the different spaces of learning that exist for our students.

Reports such as OECD Future of Education 2030 challenge us to consider ways to make PE dynamic and a reality for schools (OECD, 2018). It discusses, among many other topic areas, about the need to address curriculum gaps by 'align(ing) goals, pedagogies and assessments, in particular using ICT as an opportunity for enhanced pedagogies and innovative assessment' (p. 84). We believe that FL provides a mechanism for beginning to consider these opportunities, successes of which we have seen documented in other subject areas. However, the opportunities and applications for practice within the context of PE we felt could be addressed by this book. In the chapters that follow, we delve into many of the opportunities and applications for FL in PE. We use insight from other fields, evidence from FL studies conducted in PE, as well as clues from our own practice to describe how FL might

DOI: 10.4324/9781003203377-1

be able to support quality PE outcomes across different domains of learning. We also offer considerations to help teachers decide if FL is right for their context and iterative, progressive implementation strategies for teachers who think FL may be a suitable approach to integrate into their programs.

Before that, we seek to explore some of the key terms that we use throughout the book. Where appropriate, we have provided our own interpretations and definitions of these terms.

Key terms and definitions

Flipped Learning (FL) – We identify FL as a pedagogical approach used by educators that occurs before and during face-to-face classes. It works with the format of using asynchronous (digital) instruction to prime and inform student understanding. In chapter 10 (the conclusion), we propose a definition of FL for physical education.

Physical Education (PE) – The title of the school subject in which planned and progressive learning takes place. This includes 'learning to move' and 'moving to learn'.

Digital Technology – For us, this means any software, hardware, or network that has a digital or computerised basis. These include examples such as iPads, smartphones, and websites. These are also commonly referred to as Information and Communication Technologies (ICT).

Pedagogy – We use the definition provided by Kirk et al. (2006, p. xi) and refer to pedagogy as the combination of the three elements of teaching, learning, and curriculum.

Curriculum – This book uses the term to describe legislation texts regarding PE on national, regional, or local level, e.g., the national curriculum in PE in Norway.[1]

Student – We use the term student to cover the individuals attending an educational context. That might span individuals attending primary school to higher education.

Guiding Principles – A proposition that serves as a foundation for our thinking behind FL and guides our practice.

Preflection – Our understanding of preflection is based in the works of MaKinster et al. (2006) and Wu et al. (2015) who describe this phenomenon as a form of *reflection-for-action* as contrasted with reflection-in-action and reflection-on-action that guides future action based on past thoughts and actions.

Chapter overviews

Chapter 1: Introduction to flipped learning in physical education

In this chapter, we offer the context and rationale behind this book. We briefly discuss a synopsis of each of the chapters and give an overview of what you can expect as you move throughout the contents. It will also define key terms used in the book (e.g., curriculum, flipped learning) to create a shared understanding.

Part I: Opportunities for flipped learning in physical education

Chapter 2: 'Global' physical education

This chapter explores some of the main features or ambitions for physical education that exist globally. For example, it considers questions such as, what are some of the main (and perhaps contested) purposes of physical education? What outcomes are physical educators trying to achieve for their students? What challenges exist for physical education internationally? Given the context of flipped learning, this chapter also briefly explores the role of online and digital technology in education, and physical education more specifically. Alongside these goals, this chapter attends to the global pedagogical trends in physical education in order to lead into the third chapter which explores how flipped learning is defined in detail – questioning, how does it fit in with broader educational trends and pedagogical approaches in education and physical education?

Chapter 3: Flipped learning in (physical) education

This chapter considers what is currently recognised as flipped learning both outside and inside the physical education context. We investigate key features in terms of seeking to define flipped learning, its boundaries, and its format. In chapter 10, we will from this starting point propose a (tentative) definition of flipped learning in physical education.

Chapter 4: Flipped learning and physical activity

This chapter explores some of the reasons why educators and practitioners may choose to use flipped learning to support physical activity opportunities. It will explain how the approach might improve the quality of face-to-face physical education as well as promote engagement outside of class using the Theory of Expanded, Extended, and Enhanced Opportunities for Youth Physical Activity Promotion (Beets et al., 2016). An overview of how flipped learning can be used to support whole school approaches to physical activity promotion is also provided.

Chapter 5: Flipped learning and learning

This chapter explores flipped learning and what type of learning this pedagogical approach supports. For example, the concepts of surface and deep learning are investigated, and we attend to the role of the teacher in promoting learning. What is relevant is the shift from thinking solely about activity in PE to thinking about learning in PE. This enhancement in learning is understood and explained through situated learning, cooperative learning, and the design-oriented didactical theory lenses.

Chapter 6: Flipped learning and motivation

This chapter explores the flipped learning approach and its relation to addressing and improving motivation. Self-determination theory and expectancy-value theory are used to explain and understand this change in motivation and to underpin our arguments that FL seems to benefit all students regarding motivation in PE. Topics like contextualisation and autonomy are discussed alongside gender, age, and school level.

Part II: Applications of flipped learning in physical education

Chapter 7: When flipped learning ambition meets physical education tradition

This chapter explores some of the ambitions and theoretical underpinnings behind flipped learning, how they can be interpreted, and considerations for implementation in practice. It considered aspects such as motivations, preparations, learning environments, and cultures. Some of the challenges and common obstacles of putting our ambitions of flipped learning into practice are discussed before bringing together some of the support strategies that can aid educators in addressing or overcoming such challenges.

Chapter 8: Guiding principles for flipped learning in a variety of contexts

This chapter explores some of the guiding principles to consider when implementing high-quality flipped learning in practice. Using three case studies from the author's contexts (the UK, United States, and Norway), we explore the different variations in using flipped learning in physical education to attend to different learning outcomes.

Chapter 9: How do I start with flipped learning in physical education, and where could it lead?

This chapter maps out flipped learning starting points for teachers to consider as they begin or continue to implement the approach. We offer step-by-step strategies and considerations that can be used to guide progressive implementation of flipped learning from a single class to incorporating it within a whole physical education course. It is meant to stimulate potential users of the approach to begin thinking about ways they can deploy reflective, exploratory, and impactful uses of flipped learning to begin developing and applying their interpretations of the approach.

Chapter 10: Towards a definition of flipped learning in physical education – summary and concluding thoughts

This chapter will conclude by presenting a summary of the topics covered and key arguments discussed within them. Each of the authors considers some concluding thoughts of ways in which the ideas presented can be taken forward and the next steps for practitioners, teachers, and researchers to consider. This includes a working definition of flipped learning in physical education.

We have written this book in a manner by which you can read any chapter in isolation if you wish. Whether you are interested in the opportunities, application, or both parts of this book, we hope the content guides you through the use of flipped learning in physical education and supports you in your practice journey with flipped learning.

Note

1 https://www.udir.no/lk20/kro01-05?lang=eng

References

Beets, M. W., Okely, A., Weaver, R. G., Webster, C., Lubans, D., Brusseau, T., Carson, R., & Cliff, D. P. (2016). The theory of expanded, extended, and enhanced opportunities for youth physical activity promotion. *International Journal of Behavioral Nutrition and Physical Activity, 13*(1), 1–15. doi:10.1186/s12966-016-0442-2

Castelli, D., & Rink, J. (2003). A comparison of high and low performing secondary physical education programs. *Journal of Teaching in Physical Education, 22*(5), 512–532.

Daum, D. N., & Buschner, C. (2014). Research on teaching blended and online physical education. In R. E. Ferdig & K. Kennedy (Eds.), *Handbook of research on K-12 online and blended learning* (1st ed., pp. 201–222). Carnegie Mellon University: ETC Press.

Daum, D. N., & Buschner, C. (2018). Research on teaching K-12 online physical education. In R. E. Ferdig & K. Kennedy (Eds.), *Handbook of research on K-12 online and blended learning* (2nd ed., pp. 321–334). Carnegie Mellon University: ETC Press.

Killian, C. M., Kinder, C. J., & Woods, A. M. (2019). Online and blended instruction in K–12 physical education: A scoping review. *Kinesiology Review, 8*(2), 110–129. doi:10.1123/kr.2019-0003

Killian, C. M., Trendowski, T. N., & Woods, A. M. (2016). Students' perceptions of flipped instruction in a university physical activity course. 2016 AIESEP International Conference, Laramie, WY, USA.

Kirk, D., Macdonald, D., & O'Sullivan, M. (2006). *The handbook of physical education*. Sage.

MaKinster, J., Barab, S., Harwood, W., & Andersen, H. (2006). The effect of social context on the reflective practice of preservice science teachers: Incorporating a web-supported community of teachers. *Journal of technology and teacher education, 14*(3), 543–579.

OECD. (2018). *The future of education and skills: Education 2030*. O. Publishing. doi:10.1787/9789264239555-en

Sargent, J., & Casey, A. (2020). Flipped learning, pedagogy and digital technology: Establishing consistent practice to optimise lesson time. *European Physical Education Review, 26*, 70–84. doi:10.1177/1356336X19826603

Wu, L., Ye, X., & Looi, C.-K. (2015). Teachers' preflection in early stages of diffusion of an innovation. *Journal of Computers in Education, 2*(1), 1–24. doi:10.1007/s40692-014-0022-x

Part I

Opportunities in Flipped Learning in Physical Education

2 'Global' Physical Education

Purposes of PE

There have been longstanding and ongoing discussions within the field of physical education (PE) around what the purpose or aims of PE are or should be. Indeed, given the variations in how PE is taught, governed (i.e., by curriculum), and positioned across the globe, the lack of consensus is perhaps unsurprising. These variations have also been discussed at a variety of distinct levels such as teachers, students, government, and the media. However, much of the richness in practices or experiences of PE arises due to this variation. Therefore, we do have to question whether there is a need to have a consensus as to the goals and purposes of PE across the globe and what would we lose because of a uniform approach to PE.

David Kirk and Ken Green are some of the many scholars who have written about what some of the contested focuses of PE have been (and in many ways continue) to occur. For example, Kirk (2010) has been vocal in the viewpoint of PE being used as a vehicle to teach sport techniques. This 'sportified' approach to PE is often seen to influence both boys and girls in different ways (you can read more about this in Chapters 5 and 6). Similarly, he also discussed the goal of PE to motivate all students to engage in a lifelong physical active and healthy lifestyle (Kirk, 2010). Others have focused on the view of PE as synonymous with physical activity and as a vehicle to increase students' heart rates and their levels of activity. This view of PE's purpose is often viewed through its role in public health – such as PE preparing children for a lifetime of physical activity. If one sees these elements as the purposes of PE, then the 'physical' part of PE becomes comes to the fore. There is not much of a focus on areas such as cognitive, affective, or social learning (Bailey et al., 2009). Several scholars have argued that both students and their teachers find it difficult to explicit

DOI: 10.4324/9781003203377-3

what students are supposed to learn in PE (Siedentop, 2002). See Chapter 5 for further elaboration on how learning is seen upon in PE and how flipped learning (FL) can affect this learning. Yet, as Quennerstedt (2019b) has recently put forward, the educational part (the 'E') in PE is arguably in danger of becoming an undertaking of sport, fitness instruction, physical activity facilitation, or obesity prevention.

When we take the perspectives of PE teachers into account, studies have shown that the overarching purpose of PE was centred on the subject preparing young people for a lifetime of physical activity (McEvoy et al., 2017). Conversely, at a primary level in Ireland, educators' understanding of the purpose of PE was related to health and physical activity (Murphy & McEvoy, 2020). In the Swedish context, some have argued there is a blur in relation to a difficulty in identifying specific movement cultures such as physical training, sports, or dance (Larsson & Karlefors, 2015). Taking these perspectives into account, we see a consideration of the physical element of PE in terms of health-related exercise and physical fitness.

When we look at the purpose of PE and who it is for, then young people and their learning come to the fore. When asking young people in England what they thought about the nature and purposes of PE were about, we see focus on fun, enjoyment, and social interaction with peers (Smith & Parr, 2007). In Norway, we see views of PE as a break from other school lessons (Lyngstad et al., 2019) and the subject is one of the most popular as chosen by students. In this regard, the social and affective elements of PE are highlighted.

Finally, the government plays a role in considering the purpose and nature of PE. This often changes over time to consider new priorities, perspectives, or foci. One way in which the government is involved in perspectives regarding the purposes of PE is through National Curricula. As Kirk (2019) argues, debates surrounding national curricula continue to question and illuminate the degree in which school PE in terms of its nature, form, and content has been subject to debate. Considering the ways curricula are used internationally, we can see a variety of differences in the purposes of PE. For example, in Australia, health is a large focus and encompasses aspects such as developing health literacy. Conversely in Brazil and Portugal, there is argued to be a focus on three key skills which included operational, conceptual, and attitudinal skill development (Lavoura & Neves, 2019). Sport Policy is another aspect that the government has a relationship with PE. In the context of the UK, we see policy influencing funding but also areas for development such as the role of sports, teachers, and sports clubs.

Taking these perspectives into account, there is indeed much to be said about the role of the teacher in interpreting either the curriculum or national goals and delivering PE in relation to their own beliefs and philosophies around the value and purposes of the subject, particularly in contexts such as the United States where education is localised and there is minimal curricular oversight. Similarly, these beliefs are not static. They are multifaceted, and may change over time as they are disrupted or reflected upon by the teacher.

What could be summarised from the above is that, globally, the purpose of PE is learning to find meaning in movement. Arguably, the common factors are some kinds of movement or aspects of physical activity. However, the meaning that is given to PE is determined by the outcomes which are in focus and which kinds of movement are considered legitimate, e.g., health, cognitive processes, or sports (Kirk, 2010; Svennberg, 2017). We look at these in the next section where we consider the different educational outcomes for PE and some of the challenges associated with them (aspects of physical activity are covered in Chapter 4).

Educational outcomes and challenges

Health-related learning

The relationship between health and PE has not been a topic of much debate and critique (Cale et al., 2020). Given that there are vast spaces in which learning can take place both within and beyond the formal boundaries of the school, the aspect of health and students' understanding of health is varied. For example, as Goodyear et al. (2019) have explored, young people are likely to use both digital and non-digital spaces as sources of information regarding health. These include the sources of apps and wearable devices but also family members and peers. Topics of focus might include the number of steps taken or heart rate. Or as Quennerstedt (2019a) fittingly states:

> Globally, health has been advocated as a major objective for physical education, and despite the multiple ways that health can be understood, a specific mantra seemingly dominates Western physical education contexts in terms of health being connected to aerobic capacity, fitness, Body Mass Index, 10,000 steps per day, or body shape.
>
> (p. 2)

Additionally, there is a diversity in how health is positioned in relation to the role of PE. For example, as Armour and Harris (2013) have argued, internationally there is an uncertainty regarding the role of PE in health and the levels of responsibility for addressing health-related outcomes. This is further exacerbated by health policy and curriculum expectations in different national and local contexts. As such, the role of PE in supporting or addressing health-related learning is a challenge for PE both inside and outside the context of digital technology. Rather than confining health and health education to the prevention of premature death and disease, health must be positioned in relation to learning, as always being in the process of becoming (Quennerstedt, 2019a). We argue that PE needs to take an ever greater role in supporting students with knowledge on how to critically acquire health-related information online, especially through social media as there are reports on how those medias have negative impact on youth health (Royal Society for Public Health, 2017).

Outsourcing

Outsourcing can be characterised as the merging of provisions in-between private and public services and an external (to the school) provision of PE. In the context of PE, this could include bringing in an external company into the school to deliver football coaching. Outsourcing can pose a challenge to PE (particularly so in a primary or elementary setting) but also offers opportunities for the subject (Sperka, 2020; Sperka & Enright, 2018). Whipp et al. (2011), for example, show how generalist PE teachers reported enhanced confidence and skills regarding their ability to effectively instruct PE after a 6-month externally provided physical activity programme. Others such as Macdonald et al. (2020) have argued that there are power relations at play around aspects such as the governance of health and the financial constraints of such programmes. In relation to FL, the interplay of technologies and companies who create and develop aspects such as apps, programmes, or videos as sources of PE is an aspect of FL whereby outsourcing could become a concern.

Sport

Traditional forms of structured sport such as clubs and activities remain significant for many children. Yet the term 'sport' has become synonymous with several aspects of informal and formal types of physical activity, for example, 'lifestyle sports,' 'extreme sports', or 'serious leisure' (O'Connor & Penney, 2021). The involvement of diverse types of sport within the confines of PE at school has been used often to teach specific skills which are embedded within the sports themselves. Indeed, the Sport Education Model uses sports as the basis of its focus. Yet, as colleagues such as Hastie and Mesquita (2017) point out, sports-based approaches have been traditionally taught to be competitive which can exclude the participation of students who may not have the knowledge and skills to successfully participate or who are not interested in sports (Solmon, 2021). As such, the amount of focus on sport (in and of itself) or sport as a vehicle for developing knowledge and skills remains an educational outcome for the field (and you!) to consider.

Pedagogical 'trends'

In PE, there have been a variety of different pedagogical approaches used. Indeed, Casey and Kirk (2020) make the case for models-based practice and make a case for the term pedagogical model. Taking the above areas to account, when sports and games are the focus, pedagogical models such as Sport Education, Game Sense, or Teaching Games for Understanding could be used (Aggerholm et al., 2018). When health is the focus, some used but, less known than the above, models used include Health Optimizing Physical Education or Sports, Play and Active Recreation for Kids (SPARK). Others such as Haerens et al. (2011) argue for Health-Based Physical Education (HBPE). While it is not our intention in this book to compare FL in relation to any of these other pedagogical models or approaches, we wanted to acknowledge that there are indeed a wide variety of different approaches that are already used within PE (e.g., Cooperative Learning – Chapter 5). Indeed, as this book will cover, FL is an approach that we believe can contribute towards our pedagogical repertoires and can be complimentary to rather than replace any of our existing approaches.

Online and digital technology in PE

The role of online and digital technology in the teaching and learning of PE has been developing over the past decade or so. While we might not see the use of overhead projectors or TVs rolled out on a trolley anymore, the use of Virtual Learning Environments, video for analysis and feedback as well as the use of apps on devices such as iPads are more commonplace. For example, Casey and Jones (2011) reported on the use of video to support student engagement and we are still seeing examples such as Kok et al. (2020) and Lin et al. (2022) reporting on the use of video in PE to support feedback and learning opportunities. Given the focus on movement in PE, the ability to capture, re-watch, analyse, and discuss the content of a video provides a useful tool for exploring many aspects of PE.

Nonetheless, the use of digital technology within schools and subsequently within PE is varied. It depends on the setup of the school, the number of devices available, the option for students to bring their own devices (BYOD). There are also differences in terms of the types of technologies which are used. For example, one might expect to see more synchronous technologies such as instant chat or a shared whiteboard being used during face-to-face PE. Yet, at home, PE is likely to be experienced through online and asynchronous technologies such as a forum, recorded lecture, or email. As Whitehead (2020) argues the role of schools and schooling in education and PE is indeed of importance given the role of schools, teachers, and government. Therefore, digital technology and its use in PE are not only influenced by the areas mentioned earlier but also the various actors and contexts in which it is a part.

The COVID-19 pandemic demonstrated one of the many examples of the different spaces beyond the gymnasium or sports field where PE takes place. Many schools turned to delivering PE online to students via videos or 'live' lessons. Others sought to embed PE into the daily lives of students by combining PE with recreational activity such as walking, cycling, or running or turning to 'theory-based PE' instead of 'practical PE'. In the UK, the increased media attention around Joe Wicks (a British Fitness Coach) resulted in the creation of 'PE with Joe' where free workouts aimed at children and their families were live streamed via YouTube. Some of these activities were set as a sort of 'homework' activity for students to complete while being home-schooled. Some might call this 'active' homework (Williams et al., 2013).

While the use of homework in PE may not be commonplace (Hill, 2018; Novak & Lynott, 2015), the use of digital technologies to largen the boundaries between learning inside and outside of school. Using the Internet, this has resulted in students being able to access learning platforms, systems, and learning materials from their homes. Given the proposed benefits highlighted in the literature in terms of homework in PE promoting knowledge development, physical activity (Hill, 2018), we feel that the combination of digital technology with in-class and home-based learning has been underexplored. Subsequently, FL, a concept that we explore in more detail in the next chapter, allows us to further unpick and expand the connections between digital technology, different educational outcomes, and meet our goals for the purposes of PE.

This chapter has sought to highlight the main purposes of PE that exist globally to contextualise the subject in which is the focus of this book. It has considered some of the purposes of PE which include physical activity and lifelong learning. It touched upon some of the educational outcomes that are the focus of PE such as health and sports and considers some of the challenges embedded in these foci. It finished with a brief discussion of online and digital technologies in PE before considering the notion of homework.

Questions for reflection

- What do you see as some of the main goals or purposes for PE?
- How do digital technologies and homework fit with these purposes?
- What educational outcomes do you seek to support your students towards achieving and have these changed over time?

References

Aggerholm, K., Standal, O., Barker, D., & Larsson, H. (2018). On practising in physical education: Outline for a pedagogical model. *Physical Education and Sport Pedagogy*, *23*(2), 197–208. doi:10.1080/17408989.2017.1372408

Armour, K., & Harris, J. (2013). Making the case for developing new PE-for-health pedagogies. *Quest*, *65*(2), 201–219. doi:10.1080/00336297.2013.773531

Bailey, R., Armour, K., Kirk, D., Jess, M., Pickup, I., Sandford, R., Education, B. P., & Sport Pedagogy Special Interest Group. (2009). The educational benefits claimed for physical education and school sport: An academic review. *Research Papers in Education*, *24*(1), 1–27. doi:10.1080/02671520701809817

Cale, L., Harris, J., & Hooper, O. (2020). Get (ting) to the start line–the evaluation of an innovative intervention to address adolescents' school-related stress and anxiety. *European Physical Education Review*, *26*(3), 642–663. doi:10.1177/1356336X20902487

Casey, A., & Jones, B. (2011). Using digital technology to enhance student engagement in physical education. *Asia-Pacific Journal of Health, Sport and Physical Education*, *2*(2), 51–66. doi:10.1080/18377122.2011.9730351

Casey, A., & Kirk, D. (2020). *Models-based practice in physical education.* Routledge.

Goodyear, V. A., Armour, K. M., & Wood, H. (2019). Young people learning about health: The role of apps and wearable devices. *Learning, Media and Technology*, *44*(2), 193–210. doi:10.1080/17439884.2019.1539011

Haerens, L., Kirk, D., Cardon, G., & De Bourdeaudhuij, I. (2011). Toward the development of a pedagogical model for health-based physical education. *Quest*, *63*(3), 321–338. doi:10.1080/00336297.2011.10483684

Hastie, P. A., & Mesquita, I. (2017). Sport-based physical education. In C.D. Ennis (Ed.), *Routledge handbook of physical education pedagogies* (pp. 68–84). Routledge.

Hill, K. (2018). Homework in physical education? A review of physical education homework literature. *Journal of Physical Education, Recreation & Dance*, *89*, 58–63. doi:10.1080/07303084.2018.1440263

Kirk, D. (2010). *Physical education futures.* Routledge.

Kirk, D. (2019). *Precarity, critical pedagogy and physical education.* Routledge.

Kok, M., Komen, A., van Capelleveen, L., & van der Kamp, J. (2020). The effects of self-controlled video feedback on motor learning and self-efficacy in a physical education setting: An exploratory study on the shot-put. *Physical Education and Sport Pedagogy*, *25*(1), 49–66. doi:10.1080/17408989.2019. 1688773

Larsson, H., & Karlefors, I. (2015). Physical education cultures in Sweden: Fitness, sports, dancing … learning? *Sport, Education and Society*, *20*(5), 573–587. doi:10.1080/13573322.2014.979143

Lavoura, T. N., & Neves, R. (2019). The educational purposes of Physical Education-curricular dialogues between Brazil and Portugal. *Motriz: Revista de Educação Física*, *25*(2). doi:10.1590/S1980-6574201900020002

Lin, Y.-N., Hsia, L.-H., & Hwang, G.-J. (2022). Fostering motor skills in physical education: A mobile technology-supported ICRA flipped learning model. *Computers & Education*, *177*, 1–16. doi:10.1016/j.compedu.2021.104380

Lyngstad, I., Bjerke, Ø., & Lagestad, P. (2019). Students' views on the purpose of physical education in upper secondary school. Physical education as a break in everyday school life – learning or just fun? *Sport, Education and Society*, 1–12. doi:10.1080/13573322.2019.1573421

Macdonald, D., Johnson, R., & Lingard, B. (2020). Globalisation, neoliberalisation, and network governance: An international study of outsourcing in health and physical education. *Discourse: Studies in the Cultural Politics of Education*, *41*(2), 169–186. doi:10.1080/01596306.2020.1722422

McEvoy, E., Heikinaro-Johansson, P., & MacPhail, A. (2017). Physical education teacher educators' views regarding the purpose(s) of school physical education. *Sport, Education and Society*, *22*(7), 812–824. doi:10.1080/135 73322.2015.1075971

Murphy, F., & McEvoy, E. (2020). Listening to the voices of teachers: Primary physical education in Ireland. *Sport in Society*, *23*(8), 1320–1336. doi:10. 1080/17430437.2020.1769953

Novak, B. E., & Lynott, F. J. (2015). Homework in physical education: Benefits and implementation. *Strategies, 28*(1), 22–26. doi:10.1080/08924562.2014.980873

O'Connor, J., & Penney, D. (2021). Informal sport and curriculum futures: An investigation of the knowledge, skills and understandings for participation and the possibilities for physical education. *European Physical Education Review, 27*(1), 3–26. doi:10.1177/1356336X20915937

Quennerstedt, M. (2019a). Healthying physical education - on the possibility of learning health. *Physical Education and Sport Pedagogy, 24*(1), 1–15. doi:10.1080/17408989.2018.1539705

Quennerstedt, M. (2019b). Physical education and the art of teaching: Transformative learning and teaching in physical education and sports pedagogy. *Sport, Education and Society, 24*(6), 611–623. doi:10.1080/13573322.2019.1574731

Royal Society for Public Health. (2017). *Status of mind: Social media and young people's mental health.* https://rsph.org.uk/static/uploaded/d125b27c-0b62-41c5-a2c0155a8887cd01.pdf

Siedentop, D. (2002). Content knowledge for physical education. *Journal of Teaching in Physical Education, 21*, 368–377.

Smith, A., & Parr, M. (2007). Young people's views on the nature and purposes of physical education: A sociological analysis. *Sport, Education and Society, 12*(1), 37–58. doi:10.1080/13573320601081526

Solmon, M. A. (2021). Physical education and sport pedagogy: The application of the academic discipline of kinesiology. *Kinesiology Review, 10*(3), 331–338. doi:10.1123/kr.2021-0026

Sperka, L. (2020). (Re)defining outsourcing in education. *Discourse: Studies in the Cultural Politics of Education*, 1–13. doi:10.1080/01596306.2020.1722429

Sperka, L., & Enright, E. (2018). The outsourcing of health and physical education: A scoping review. *European Physical Education Review, 24*(3), 349–371. doi:10.1177/1356336X17699430

Svennberg, L. (2017). Swedish PE teachers' understandings of legitimate movement in a criterion-referenced grading system. *Physical Education and Sport Pedagogy, 22*(3), 257–269. doi:10.1080/17408989.2016.1176132

Whipp, P. R., Hutton, H., Grove, J.R., & Jackson, B. (2011). Outsourcing physical education in primary schools: Evaluating the impact of externally provided programmes on generalist teachers. *Asia-Pacific Journal of Health, Sport and Physical Education, 2*(2), 67–77. doi:10.1080/18377122.2011.9730352

Whitehead, M. (2020). The nature of physical education. In S. Capel, J. Cliffe, & J. Lawrence (Eds.), *A practical guide to teaching physical education in the secondary school* (3rd ed., pp. 6–16). Routledge.

Williams, S. M., McGladrey, B. W., Silva, A., & Hannon, J. C. (2013). Comparison of classroom instruction versus use of homework assignments on cognitive knowledge acquisition in physical education. *Physical Educator, 70*(2), 206–220.

3 Flipped Learning in (Physical) Education

All students deserve access to quality physical education (PE) opportunities that support their engagement in meaningful, enriching movement experiences. PE primarily emphasises learning within the psychomotor (e.g., fundamental motor skill development) domain making it the only subject where students engage in instructional physical activity opportunities during the school day (Erwin et al., 2013). In combination with participation in meaningful psychomotor experiences, engagement with cognitive and affective content forms a foundation for learning in PE. Students' PE experiences at each level of schooling can influence their knowledge, skills, and beliefs about physical activity, which can ultimately impact their activity levels into adulthood (Ennis, 2010; Ladwig et al., 2018). Therefore, it is essential that students have access to high-quality learning opportunities in PE across their primary and secondary schooling tenures. Unfortunately, students' access to quality PE opportunities varies across the globe and is largely dependent on national, regional, or local policies. These policies often determine the number of days students attend school-based PE, the amount of time allotted for PE participation, the number of students attending class, the makeup of curriculums, and the provision of space and equipment, for example. Given the generally unsupportive nature of PE policies globally (Marshall & Hardman, 2000; Penney, 2013; Society of Health and Physical Educators [SHAPE] America, 2016), many students' opportunities are restricted and negatively impacted through the erosion of PE time or days (Castelli & Rink, 2003). Limited time to achieve the curriculum represents a significant problem for numerous PE teachers. In many countries, expecting students to develop deep knowledge, positive attitudes towards physical activity, and develop motor competence is arguably unrealistic given the current limitations and constraints being placed on PE teachers. In other words, it has become difficult for teachers to teach their whole curriculums (deeply) and therefore it has become

DOI: 10.4324/9781003203377-4

challenging for students to work at progressing towards broad outcomes beyond physical activity engagement, such as skill-based, knowledge, and affective learning. Nevertheless, national curriculums and learning standards reflect expectations for students to be able to demonstrate learning within all three learning domains.

While it remains essential to continue to advocate for supportive policies and adequate curriculum time, seeking alternative avenues for increasing program impact becomes necessary to overcome current barriers, preserve contact time with students, and ensure all students have access to adequate, high-quality learning opportunities regardless of their PE contexts and environments. Since teachers are often not in charge of designating curriculum time and making other policy decisions, key questions for PE teachers to then ask might be as follows:

- How can I create conditions that will allow adequate, deep learning opportunities to occur for my students (without relying on external decision-makers)?
- What tools can I utilise and optimise to gain learning time for my subject and students?

The flipped learning (FL) approach represents one teacher-directed option that may help PE teachers overcome barriers to quality PE to expand and enhance the learning opportunities in their classes. FL can broaden the boundaries of PE instruction through the use of asynchronous (digital) instruction. By integrating an asynchronous (on-demand, independent) digital instructional component to PE through FL, teachers can effectively eliminate time constraints of the PE class period and the need for geographic proximity of the gym/field/pool (Sun et al., 2008). This occurs by offering instruction *outside of class*, thereby potentially increasing the amount of (active) learning time accessible to students *in class.* In other words, FL may give teachers freedom to finally get what they want- time, and opportunities to teach more deeply regardless of their current constraints and without relying on external decision-makers. While other strategies to enhance learning in PE rely exclusively on in-class methods (e.g., better routines, instructional models), FL allows for the expansion of learning beyond the class period and school building.

FL defined

FL originated and was developed within classroom-based subjects as a way to support student learning and integrate social collaborative educational approaches (Bates et al., 2017; Bishop & Verleger, 2013). It is an instructional approach that is often referred to interchangeably as 'inverted', 'blended', or 'hybrid' instruction. While these teaching strategies may overlap with FL, there are some defining features that distinguish FL from flipped, inverted, blended, or hybrid *classrooms* or *instruction*. For example, many teachers might assume that assigning an article to read or video for students to watch before class, then discussing it during class, qualifies as FL. Early on, FL was conceptualised more as a flipped classroom teaching *format* where 'events that have traditionally taken place inside the classroom now take place outside the classroom and vice versa' (Lage et al., 2000, p. 32). However, the FL approach goes beyond what we might call traditional 'homework', which the example represents. As the approach evolved, FL became recognised as a way to support and emphasise student-centred learning approaches like peer teaching and cooperative learning (Bates et al., 2017; Bishop & Verleger, 2013) and has emerged as a means to support integration of learning technology (Hotle & Garrow, 2016).

Current consensus is building around the Flipped Learning Network (FLN) definition of FL, which characterises the approach beyond simply a way to format instruction. Instead, the FLN (2014) explains FL as:

> A pedagogical approach in which direct instruction moves from the group learning space to the individual learning space and the resulting group space is transformed into a dynamic, interactive learning environment where the educator guides students as they apply concepts and engage creatively in the subject matter.
>
> (Flipped Learning Network [FLN], 2014, p. 1)

In other words, the main feature of FL is not just the use of asynchronous digital instruction, although this aspect is essential. Instead, it is the focus on student-centred pedagogies and away from teacher-directed instruction that sets FL apart from flipped, blended, or inverted classroom formats (Bergmann & Sams, 2014). The student-centred approach to teaching before and during face-to-face classes is supported by the format of using asynchronous (digital) instruction to prime or inform student understanding.

The use of FL contrasts traditional teacher-centred direct instruction or lecture-based approaches by offering foundational course content outside of the classroom, using digital technologies (Mason et al., 2013). The asynchronous, on-demand nature of digital content delivery allows students to self-pace their engagement with course material prior to in-class application. Previewing new information and skills through well-defined, self-regulated digital instruction before class supports students in their preparation for in-class applied learning activities ahead of time (Giannakos et al., 2016). Student-centred, guided-learning opportunities aligned with the digital content are then facilitated by teachers during subsequent classes to encourage students to apply their knowledge and skills in face-to-face learning experiences (Hawks, 2014), often through cooperative or self-paced activities. This shift to more student-centred approaches requires adjustment in the role of the FL teacher towards being more of a facilitator or knowledge-broker (Macdonald, 2015) rather than a dispenser of information (Barbour & Kennedy, 2014). Or to use a phrase common to some, the teacher using FL should become more of a 'guide on the side' rather than a 'sage on the stage'.

Current learning technologies (e.g., EdPuzzle and YouTube) allow for the distribution of high-quality digital content, like teacher-created or teacher-curated videos, through a diverse range of forms, such as mobile devices, tablets, and computers. Many schools across the primary and secondary spectrum also integrate learning management systems (LMSs) into their daily function as a digital space for communicating with students, guardians, and organising digital learning experiences. Within an FL environment, teachers can leverage the tools available through schools' LMSs to implement the digital aspect of the course, like posting video content, distributing, and collecting assignments, or conducting assessments. Teachers who work in schools that do not employ LMSs can use freely available systems like Google Classrooms to organise the digital contents within the digital components of their FL approach.

FL format

The instructional format of FL is in many ways different than traditional teaching methods because it requires the delivery of content prior to class and focuses on student-centred knowledge and skill application during class. This is illustrated in Figure 3.1.

The two large squares at the bottom of the graphic represent in-school, face-to-face PE classes. Both traditional and flipped PE leverage face-to-face classes for the purposes of promoting student learning. The lines of these squares are solid to signify the fixed space (at school) and time (during a predetermined block of time) of a face-to-face PE class period. Each solid face-to-face class square contains

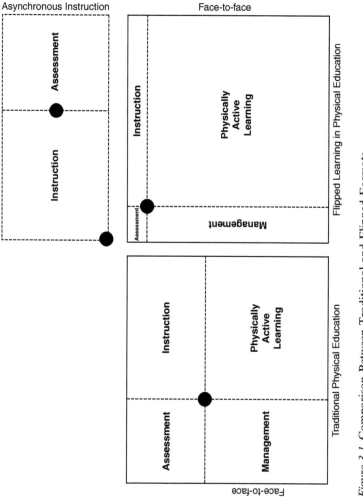

Figure 3.1 Comparison Between Traditional and Flipped Formats.

some of the general components of regular PE classes (i.e., instruction, student management, assessment, and active learning). These components are represented by dotted lines to represent the fluid, interrelated and teacher and student-directed nature of face-to-face class components during a given class period. For example, the amount of time a teacher spends managing students may fluctuate depending on the content of a lesson. For example, archery instruction and practice likely require more management time than indoor basketball due to the need for students to adhere to strict safety protocol to avoid serious injury during archery. As management fluctuates, it can impact the amount of physical activity or skill practice available to students (i.e., more time spent in management might mean less time spent in skill practice opportunities). Conversely, during days when there is a knowledge assessment, there may be less time for instruction and physical activity in the same way there may be less time needed for instruction and management time during tournament play at the culmination of a series of lessons.

FL format can assist teachers in overcoming the generally restricted nature (i.e., prescribed class times, fixed number of weekly class periods, class environment) of traditional PE classes. Using an exclusively traditional approach, a teacher can try to maximise physical activity opportunities only so much before important instructions or assessment time get reduced. This is where teachers often encounter barriers to quality PE and when the following questions become relevant. How can I create conditions (without relying on external decision-makers) that will allow adequate, deep learning opportunities to occur for my students? Or, what tools can I use and optimise to gain time for my subject and students? FL format helps teachers optimise conditions for learning and is one of the tools that allow teachers to gain time for their subject and students and the floating square in the figure above Flipped Physical Education is the key mechanism at work. The floating square in the graphic represents the asynchronous (digital) instruction component of FL format, which allows for greater range of flexibility during face-to-face classes. It gives teachers space to add active learning (physical activity, skill practice, game play) opportunities without sacrificing instruction and assessment time (since it should have already occurred online, prior to class). The floating square lines are dotted because instruction and assessment time occur outside the boundaries of the class period and school building and are therefore teacher-driven and fluid/not fixed. In other words, PE teachers decide the amount of time spent on content delivery and assessments during the asynchronous (digital) aspects of FL. When teachers plan FL well, they do not have to repeat the instruction delivered digitally during face-to-face classes, which should give more space and opportunities for physical activity engagement. This idea is expanded in Chapters 4 and 8.

FL approach

FL is defined by both the format (explained earlier) and the approach or method of using it for maximum impact. It is more than adding asynchronous (digital) instruction that corresponds to a face-to-face class (i.e., flipped, inverted, hybrid classroom). There are defining characteristics that teachers can contemplate and follow to optimise the approach beyond simply formatting their instruction differently by providing homework, then discussing it in class. To improve the impact of FL, the FLN (2014) provides four 'pillars' of the approach to guide teachers in their planning, implementation, and reflection of FL. These pillars outline some considerations for teachers thinking about flipping content in their classes and some ways in which they can ensure the classroom environment, learning culture, content, and instruction are developed in such a way that students' needs are met, and that FL occurs. A general overview of the pillars of FL is provided in Table 3.1.

These pillars represent broad, general strategies teachers can employ to guide their planning and implementation of the FL approach in their gyms and learning spaces. They illustrate the student-centred, flexible nature of learning that defines the FL approach. The FLN Pillars also show how the FL approach might deviate from standard PE environments, learning cultures, and instructional approaches (you will see more about these pillars in chapter 7).

So at this point, it might be worth asking, is FL even appropriate for PE? The following section will describe more about the general utility of the approach within PE. The rest of the book will focus on answering that question and offers commentary on the potential of FL to positively impact student physical activity, comprehensive school physical activity programming, student motivation, and deep learning. Subsequent chapters will also provide practical details on how teachers can begin to think about iteratively integrating FL into their classes and offer sequential strategies to do so reflectively.

FL in PE

What might FL look like in PE? After all, the FL approach originated in classroom-based subjects, so is the approach even appropriate for applied subjects like PE? While current research on FL has relied on

Table 3.1 Components and Strategies for Flipped Learning

Components of Flipped Learning	Strategies for Flipped Learning
Flexible environment	• Establish spaces and time frames that permit students to interact on their learning as needed • Consistently observe and monitor students to make adjustments as appropriate • Provide different ways to learn content and demonstrate mastery
Learning culture	• Give students opportunities to engage in meaningful activities without the teacher being central • Scaffold activities and make them accessible to all students through differentiation and feedback
Intentional content	• Prioritise concepts used in direct instruction for learners to access on their own • Create and/or curate relevant content (typically videos) for students • Differentiate to make content accessible and relevant to all students
Professional educator	• Be available to all students for individual, small group, and class feedback in real time as needed • Conduct ongoing formative assessments during class time through observation and by recording data to inform future instruction • Collaborate and reflect with other educators and take responsibility for transforming practice

The Four Pillars of F-L-I-P^{TM} (Flipped Learning Network [FLN], 2014)

Source: Flipped Learning Network (FLN) (2014). The Four Pillars of F-L-I-P^{TM} Reproducible PDF can be found at https://flippedlearning.org/definition-of-flipped-learning/

the FLN (2014) definition (Østerlie, 2018; Sargent & Casey, 2020), researchers within the domain of PE have been questioning this definition of and whether it fully illustrates FL within the PE context. We therefore encourage readers to take a critical position to both the definition and how it can be understood, applied, and recognised in a subject like PE (Østerlie, 2020). The following example is provided to illustrate what implementing the FL approach within an elementary PE class might look like.

There are a variety of ways in which FL can be implemented within PE. An elementary PE teacher might decide to begin using FL during a series of lessons designed around balance. They could create and post a video for students to watch with a parent or guardian before the first lesson of the series. This video might introduce the skills of balance to students by defining essential vocabulary and skill cues, explaining the value of balance, and describing its role in relation to performing other movement skills. The video might also include several demonstrations of various basic balance skills. At the end of the video, the teacher might encourage students to think of (and practice) three different ways they can balance using different parts of their bodies as anchor points. This prompt could serve as a strategy to promote student accountability to the whole video content/tasks, as well as a formative self-assessment. It might also be used to prime students for the initial activity of the upcoming face-to-face lesson. When students arrive in class, the teacher could begin the lesson with an activity designed for students to practice applying their new knowledge by sharing the three balances they created at home with various classmates as they move through general space of the learning environment. As music plays, students might perform various locomotor skills while maintaining personal space. When the music stops, students might find a (new) partner and begin to mirror each other's creative balances. Following this warm-up application, the teacher might extend students' understanding of balancing through a variety of activities, like using imagery to prompt students into new ways of balancing their bodies or introducing various objects to balance. Subsequent videos might be used to continue extending students' understanding and skill of balance by introducing balance in combination with other movement concepts and skills and prompting practice using household items, for example. The teacher might continue to design new ways for students to apply, share, peer teach, and work cooperatively during face-to-face classes to develop their balance.

The example provided above is one way in which a PE teacher might decide to implement FL in an elementary class. There are many other ways FL can be used to teach balance, let alone alternative content across elementary and secondary PE! The example in this chapter was included to demonstrate how FL is an approach that leverages an asynchronous (digital) instruction format to encourage student-centred applied learning. The teacher in the example assigned an asynchronous digital video to introduce balance and key vocabulary and cues, demonstrate basic skills, and prompt student thinking and initial practice prior to the beginning of a unit on balance. The in-class knowledge and skill practice encouraged through the video was directly applied during the class through a *student-centred* cooperative, peer teaching activity. Then the content was further developed through extension activities. Subsequent videos introduced more complex concepts and themes related to balance and applied through other in-class, *student-centred* active learning opportunities. Without the student-centred activities related to the asynchronous instruction, the FL approach would have been lost, and the value of the videos would be just like standard homework within a flipped classroom format. Several additional FL case examples from other grade levels are described in Chapter 8.

What does the research say?

When applying any pedagogical approach, there is some value in assessing its utility beyond simple observations, practical experience, or anecdotes. Decisions to use new ways of teaching should rely on experience, intuition, and the current, available research evidence base. As the upcoming chapters illustrate, FL holds a lot of potential and this conclusion is based on our years of experience using it in our own practice, as well as some hints available through recent studies. For example, a new review of research concluded that the use of FL in PE had a positive impact on a variety of student outcomes and experiences and generally benefitted students in comparison to more traditional approaches (Østerlie et al., 2021). The clearest positive impact FL had was on student motivation. However, the impact on student knowledge, motor development, and attitudes is less clear, and issues related to students' perceptions and experiences are still being explored (Killian et al., 2019). Until new studies are published indicating if and how FL might influence across a range of important outcomes, we can turn to research in other subjects, theory, and intuition based on experiences and thoughtful communications. The rest of this book will describe some potentials of FL and provide ideas about how the FL approach might be used to support student physical activity, whole school approaches to physical activity promotion, motivation, and deep learning. Our hope is that teachers use this information to decide the best use(s) (or not) of FL within their curriculums and school contexts. Indeed, the premise of this book is to propose, based upon the knowledge and experiences we currently have available, what we believe FL in PE could look like as well as offer some guidance and principles for its high-quality use. It will be up to teachers to apply a reflective approach to evaluate the best ways to use FL to support their students. What you will find in the following chapters are some of the possibilities, opportunities, and applications FL offers teachers to enhance students' PE experiences!

Questions for reflection

- How does the flipped learning format and the flipped learning approach compare?
- How does the flipped learning approach differ from traditional teaching methods in physical education?
- What barriers exist that inhibit quality physical education and how might the flipped learning approach be able to help teachers overcome these barriers?

References

Barbour, M. K., & Kennedy, K. (2014). K-12 online learning: A worldwide perspective. Paper 188. https://digitalcommons.sacredheart.edu/ced_fac/188

Bergmann, J., & Sams, A. (2014). *Flipped learning: Gateway to student engagement*. International Society for Technology in Education.

Bates, E. J., Almekdash, H., & Gilchrest-Dunnam, M. J. (2017). The flipped classroom: A brief, brief history. In L. S. Green, J. R. Banas & R. A. Perkins (Eds.), *The flipped college classroom* (pp. 3–10). Springer.

Bishop, J. L., & Verleger, M. A. (2013). The flipped classroom: A survey of the research. ASEE National Conference Proceedings, Atlanta, GA.

Castelli, D., & Rink, J. (2003). A comparison of high and low performing secondary physical education programs. *Journal of Teaching in Physical Education, 22*(5), 512–532.

Ennis, C. D. (2010). On their own: Preparing students for a lifetime. *Journal of Physical Education, Recreation & Dance, 81*(5), 17–22. doi:10.1080/07303084.2010.10598475

Erwin, H., Beighle, A., Carson, R. L., & Castelli, D. M. (2013). Comprehensive school-based physical activity promotion: A review. *Quest, 65*(4), 412–428. doi:10.1080/00336297.2013.791872

Flipped Learning Network [FLN]. (2014). *Definition of flipped learning*. Retrieved from http://flippedlearning.org/domain/46

Giannakos, M. N., Krogstie, J., & Aalberg, T. (2016). Toward a learning ecosystem to support flipped classroom: A conceptual framework and early results. In Y. Li, M. Chang, M. Kravcik, E. Popescu, R. Huang, Kinshuk, &

N.-S. Chen (Eds.), *State-of-the-art and future directions of smart learning* (pp. 105–114). Springer. doi: 10.1007/978-981-287-868-7

Hawks, S. J. (2014). The flipped classroom: Now or never? *AANA Journal, 82*, 264–269.

Hotle, S. L., & Garrow, L. A. (2016). Effects of the traditional and flipped classrooms on undergraduate student opinions and success. *Journal of Professional Issues in Engineering Education and Practice, 142*(1), 05015005. doi: 10.1061/(ASCE)EI.1943-5541.0000259

Killian, C. M., Kinder, C. J., & Woods, A. M. (2019). Online and blended instruction in K-12 physical education: A scoping review. *Kinesiology Review, 8*(2), 110–129. doi: 10.1123/kr.2019-0003

Ladwig, M. A., Vazou, S., & Ekkekakis, P. (2018). "My best memory is when I was done with it": PE memories are associated with adult sedentary behavior. *Translational Journal of the American College of Sports Medicine, 3*(16), 119–129. doi: 10.1249/TJX.0000000000000067

Lage, M. J., Platt, G. J., & Treglia, M. (2000). Inverting the classroom: A gateway to creating an inclusive learning environment. *The Journal of Economic Education, 31*(1), 30–43. doi: 10.1080/00220480009596759

Macdonald, D. (2015). Teacher-as-knowledge-broker in a futures-oriented health and physical education. *Sport, Education and Society, 20*(1), 27–41. doi: 10.1080/13573322.2014.935320

Marshall, J., & Hardman, K. (2000). The state and status of physical education in schools in international context. *European Physical Education Review, 6*(3), 203–229.

Mason, G. S., Shuman, T. R., & Cook, K. E. (2013). Comparing the effectiveness of an inverted classroom to a traditional classroom in an upper-division engineering course. *IEEE Transactions on Education, 56*(4), 430–435. doi: 10.1109/TE.2013.2249066

Østerlie, O. (2018). Can flipped learning enhance adolescents' motivation in physical education? An intervention study. *Journal for Research in Arts and Sports Education, 2*, 1–15. doi: 10.23865/jased.v2.916

Østerlie, O. (2020). *Flipped learning in physical education: A gateway to motivation and (deep) learning* [Doctoral thesis, Norwegian University of Science and Technology]. Trondheim. https://hdl.handle.net/11250/2649972

Østerlie, O., Chad, K. M., Sargent, J., Garcia-Jaen, M., Garcia-Martinez, S., & Ferriz-Valero, A. (2021). Flipped learning in physical education: A scoping review. Manuscript submitted for publication.

Penney, D. (2013). Points of tension and possibility: Boundaries in and of physical education. *Sport, Education and Society, 18*(1), 6–20. doi: 10.1080/13573322.2012.713862

Sargent, J., & Casey, A. (2020). Flipped learning, pedagogy and digital technology: Establishing consistent practice to optimise lesson time. *European Physical Education Review, 26*, 70–84. doi: 10.1177/1356336X19826603

Society of Health and Physical Educators [SHAPE] America. (2016). *SHAPE of the nation report: Status of physical education in the USA*. https://www.shapeamerica. org/advocacy/son/2016/upload/Shape-of-the-Nation-2016_web.pdf

Sun, P.-C., Tsai, R. J., Finger, G., Chen, Y.-Y., & Yeh, D. (2008). What drives a successful e-Learning? An empirical investigation of the critical factors influencing learner satisfaction. *Computers & Education, 50*(4), 1183–1202. doi:10.1016/j.compedu.2006.11.007

4 Flipped Learning and Physical Activity

Physical education and youth physical activity promotion

Flipped learning (FL) has the potential to help physical education (PE) teachers provide deep learning opportunities without sacrificing time for students to engage in meaningful movement experiences (Killian et al., 2016; Østerlie, 2020). In addition, it may provide an avenue for teachers to promote physical activity beyond the school day, as well as contribute to the enhancement of in-class instructional processes which would allow for more active learning involvement for students. These potentials are inherent in the structure of FL and made possible due to the embedded, asynchronous, digital instructional components of the approach. When teachers post content online for students to review *prior to* class, they are effectively opening time and space *during* class (when and where the instruction would have traditionally been delivered) for active learning. The capacity for FL to expand and enhance activity opportunities in PE gives teachers a tool to help them support students' knowledge growth, development of fundamental motor skills, and their progress towards engaging in the recommended 60 minutes of daily physical activity time (World Health Organization [WHO], 2020). At its core, FL represents an approach that can help teachers promote deep learning and address challenges associated with teaching PE within the current global educational climate.

Common barriers to quality PE

PE is the main school-based environment where students are provided with instructional physical activity opportunities during the school day (Erwin et al., 2013). It is also the primary context where many school-aged youths accumulate physical activity minutes (Alderman et al., 2012) and should participate in instructional motor skill development

DOI: 10.4324/9781003203377-5

(Ennis, 2011). Therefore, a primary outcome of quality PE should be student physical activity engagement. Quality programs also have the capacity to promote the development of health-related fitness knowledge (HRFK) and positive attitudes related to lifelong physical activity (Bailey, 2006), which are key components of lifelong physical activity participation (Ennis, 2010). Despite the value of quality PE and the potential for programs to positively influence student physical activity participation, it is still a marginalised subject in many countries. Education reforms also tend to prioritise language, arts, science, technology, and mathematics at the expense of PE time. As a result, this prioritisation has contributed to the erosion of the amount of PE allotted in schools across the globe (Trost & van der Mars, 2009). For example, despite recommendations by national organisations for daily PE, many students in the United States only have PE once per week during elementary schooling, 45 days during secondary schooling, or are allowed to complete PE online, during the summer (Society of Health and Physical Educators [SHAPE] America, 2016). Teachers facing these, or similar situations where there is a lack of available class time, may be prompted to compromise between providing enriching instructional experiences and offering adequate physical activity opportunities for students. The resulting dilemma might result in 'watered down' PE opportunities with instruction that promotes high amounts of student physical activity, but contains limited cognitive/ affective value (Borgen et al., 2020). Or, conversely, low student activity with robust cognitive/affective value for students. Neither scenario is ideal given the role psychomotor, cognitive, and affective development each play in students' lifelong progress toward physical literacy (Ennis, 2010). Nevertheless, it is nearly impossible for most physical educators to provide adequate opportunities for students to make appropriate gains in each of the learning domains given the limitations of school-based PE as it currently exists in its general state across the globe.

FL to support quality PE opportunities

The digital learning component embedded within the FL format can diminish the time constraints of the PE class period and the need for geographic proximity of the school for learning to occur (Sun et al., 2008). When digital instruction is employed asynchronously, as it is within the FL approach, it enables teachers to deliver in-depth instruction outside of class using the internet. This allows for the preservation and a possible increase of time for active learning opportunities in class due to a reduction in face-to-face instruction and management time (Goad et al., 2021; Killian et al., 2016; Sargent & Casey, 2020). In other words, it can help teachers address a key barrier to quality instruction-limited face-to-face class time. Students who participate in a flipped PE class can learn key information, practice skills, and engage in physical activity outside of their PE classes due to the asynchronous nature of the digital instructional component. This asynchronous feature enables students to participate in PE content before school, during study halls, at recess or breaktime, and/or after school.

Every PE class typically involves management of student behaviour and the learning environment, instruction, and physical activity components. When aspects of instruction, like skills or activity demonstrations, practice opportunity explanations, and/or organisational descriptions are placed online within FL, time spent managing and instructing students during face-to-face PE should be reduced, thereby making more room for physical activity participation since students will have already been primed to the nature of in-class activities prior to participation. In other words, when a teacher uses the digital component of FL as a priming strategy to prepare students for upcoming activities, safety expectations, or learning formations, students should already have a basic reference to class components and an understanding of expectations thereby potentially reducing the amount of time a teacher must spend redirecting and managing students into appropriate activity engagement. Instead of providing robust demonstrations or detailed directions for skill practice (since these components would have been put online), teachers using FL might conduct a brief review of the online content at the beginning of class, quickly prompt students into practice formations then spend time providing individual and small group feedback as students are engaging in active learning.

Depending on the nature of the online content and how it is employed by the teacher, digital instruction within FL could also be used as a venue to promote family and household engagement in PE practice opportunities and community support of students' PE participation. For example, a teacher might encourage students to invite a family or household member into practicing foot skills with a student in a community greenspace or creative movement challenges together in an open room. These potentials align well in support of whole school approaches to physical activity promotion, which have gained popularity in places like the United States, through the Comprehensive School Physical Activity Program model (CSPAP; Centers for Disease Control and Prevention [CDC], 2019) and Europe (Naul & Scheuer, 2020). They are also supported by the Theory of Expanded, Extended, and Enhanced Opportunities (TEO) for Youth Physical Activity Promotion (Beets et al., 2016; Killian et al., 2019; Webster et al., 2021). The rest of this chapter will focus on using the TEO as a lens to further describe the potential value of the FL approach as well as offer ideas for how PE teachers might use the approach to support whole school physical activity promotion initiatives.

A theoretical support for FL to support physical activity opportunities in PE

The TEO for Youth Physical Activity Promotion puts forth that the primary mechanisms responsible for increased physical activity within youth behavioural interventions are strategies that expand, extend, and/or enhance PE opportunities. In other words, when individuals (i.e., PE teachers) seek to promote youth physical activity within a setting (i.e., a school), approaches that expand, extend, or enhance these physical activity opportunities should be the primary consideration for planning and implementation. The FL format naturally expands (physical activity and) learning opportunities through the digital component. The TEO gives a theoretical lens through which the (potential) value of FL in PE can be discussed. It provides general language that can be applied to describe why and how FL might be able to support increased learning and physical activity opportunities through expansion and offers clues as to how it might also be able to enhance in-class physical activity opportunities in PE. Table 4.1 outlines operational definitions of the three proposed TEO mechanisms, offers general examples of each, and provides basic illustrations of how FL might apply in a PE context.

A general challenge for those seeking to expand or extend youth physical activity opportunities is they often must rely on other, external decision-makers (i.e., administrators, policymakers, and/or gatekeepers) for permission and support. For example, in most cases, PE teachers are not in a position to decide how long their classes are or how often students participate in PE per week. So, *extending* existing PE opportunities is, somewhat, out of the teachers' hands and generally dictated by the head of department, the school timetabling, or governed by the state/curriculum. Similarly, without permission and funding from administrators or community sponsors, school professionals could not reasonably *expand* traditional (i.e., non-FL) physical activity opportunities by establishing an after-school intermural sports league. *Enhancing* PE opportunities, however, is technically at the discretion of PE teachers (i.e., reducing wait time in lines, establishing and reinforcing efficient routines), but even these efforts can be limited by other barriers out of the control of the teacher such as large class sizes and/or limited space. Indeed, most PE teachers will have been in a scenario whereby part of or all the indoor spaces such as the sports hall

Table 4.1 TEO Definitions, General Examples, and Flipped Learning
Applications

TEO Mechanism	Definition	General Examples	Flipped Learning Applications
Expanded	Replacing low or sedentary activities with higher intensity activity opportunities	Substituting seatwork with "brain breaks" in general subject classrooms Opening the weight room to students before and after school	Prompting at-home practice during video instruction
Extended	Lengthening the allotted time for already allocated physical activity opportunities	Adding physical education lessons to students' weekly schedules Allocating more time for recess or breaktime	N/A to FL
Enhanced	Modifying existing physical activity opportunities to increase the amount of physical activity engagement during already allocated time	Reducing student wait time during physical education Providing choice of activities	Reducing large groups, direct instruction time

Adapted from Beets et al. (2016).

or gymnasium are used for other curricula activities such as students
sitting exams, plays or fairs. The ability of FL to naturally expand and
enhance learning in PE can therefore empower teachers to overcome
barriers independently without relying on external stakeholders.

What does FL have to do with TEO?

The format of FL can help PE teachers *expand* physical activity opportunities beyond the class period- if they strategically use their online teaching to include at-home activity promotion prompts, at-home

skill practice opportunities, and at-home physical activity-based assessments and accountability measures. In a way, expansion is a natural feature of FL. To leverage FL for the expansion of physical activity opportunities, PE teachers would need to go beyond using digital instruction to simply offer passive teaching like explaining skill cues or showing demonstrations. They would need to embed prompts into their online instruction that encourage students to be active and engage in skill practice outside of their face-to-face PE classes, which the FL allows. Figure 4.1 illustrates this by building on the figure from chapter 3 (Figure 3.1). As you can see in this chapter's updated figure, physically active learning is added as a (potential) component of the asynchronous instruction, along with instruction and assessment. Embedding at-home physical activity is not an essential feature of FL, and it may not always be appropriate to include depending on the content or school context. However, the figure demonstrates how FL can be leveraged to promote added skill practice and physical activity opportunities, if and when the teacher decides it is appropriate. The asynchronous digital format of FL allows for teacher-directed decisions about instruction and assessment. It also affords natural opportunities for teachers to promote physical activity engagement/skill practice through their videos and other digital learning materials.

Expanding physical activity opportunities with FL

If a middle school PE teacher decides to use their online instruction to introduce the basic tennis-ready position and fundamental strokes, they can *expand* physical engagement beyond the school by prompting students to find an object in their house and try practicing alternating between different stances and grips for the various strokes. A brief pause in the instructional video, with directions and cues listed on the screen, could give support to students while they complete the activity at home. A teacher might build in accountability and formative assessment by assigning students to upload a brief video of themselves doing the activity or by completing a reflective response following engagement. Teachers might also review these assignments before class to tailor their face-to-face instruction according to students' understanding.

Elementary PE teachers may use their online instruction to explain and demonstrate different ways to jump and leap. They might *expand* physical activity opportunities by encouraging students to find an open space and create different lines and shapes with a jump rope, extension cord, or a few garments of clothing. To give students a chance to try the activity, teachers might build a pause into the video after

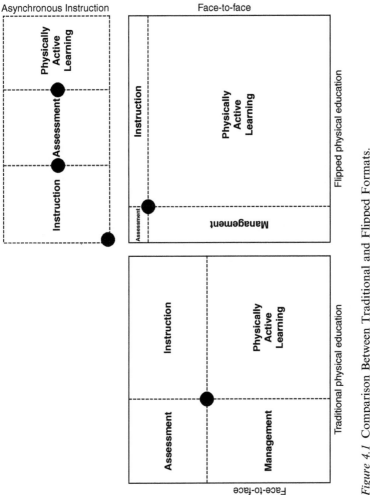

Figure 4.1 Comparison Between Traditional and Flipped Formats.

prompting students to jump in and out or around the shapes or leap over lines. To motivate students to engage in the physical activity portion of the instruction, a formative assessment could be assigned where the student uses the presented skill cues to create their own shapes and actions. Assigning students to upload several pictures or a video of the shapes and their actions could serve as the assessment artefact, in this case. These examples show how it takes intentional planning and instruction to *expand* and promote physical activity through online instruction. Without specific prompts to engage in physical activity embedded within the online component of FL, opportunities to *expand* physical activity opportunities will likely be lost.

Enhancing physical activity opportunities with FL

FL also provides a natural way for teachers to *enhance* their classes to allow for more physical activity engagement. This occurs when teachers are attentive to the content they post online and adjust the related face-to-face lesson accordingly by reducing the amount of time students spend giving direct instruction and management. In other words, teachers should use online instruction in FL to reduce the amount of time they need to spend in direct, large group instruction during class. Using the previous examples to illustrate how FL might result in the *enhancement* of physical activity opportunities, the teacher using the online instruction to teach the basic tennis grips and strokes might include a preview of upcoming skill practice opportunities students will engage in during face-to-face lessons. The preview might include organisational descriptions of the practice experiences along with video(s) depicting students or athletes of various abilities performing the activities. This should reduce the amount of time the teacher uses instructing students and organizing and managing the learning activities and there is some evidence to suggest that is likely the case (Killian et al., 2022; Østerlie et al., 2021). At the beginning of subsequent classes, instead of providing an in-depth overview of the practice activities, the teacher might ask a few key review questions and quickly prompt students into practicing since the students would already be familiar with the basic content, tasks, and formations. Once students are engaged in the activity as the teacher intends, the teacher might circulate through the learning space to provide guidance and feedback to students during the activities (Sargent & Casey, 2020). *Enhancement* of physical activity opportunities, in particular, should be a natural outcome of using FL since students should engage with most of the substantive content online, before arriving at class.

That being said, the expansion and enhancement of physical activity opportunities can only occur through intentional designing and planning. PE teachers must be strategic about promoting at-home physical activity in their video content otherwise the chance to support expanded physical activity opportunities is lost. Similarly, for enhancement of in-class opportunities to occur, teachers need to plan adequately. Their face-to-face instruction should be careful not to simply be a close repetition of the instruction delivered online. Instead, it should perhaps be limited to a brief review of the online content before prompting students into practice opportunities and game play, where further small groups and individual instruction can take place. Therefore, enhancement of in-class physical activity opportunities can only happen if teachers consider the content they posted online and adjust their in-class instructional plans accordingly. If teachers end up repeating the bulk of their online instruction during class, then there will likely be no corresponding enhancement of in-class physical activity opportunities. This of course is only effective (and safe) to do if students engage meaningfully with the online content. There are inherent issues and challenges associated with the provision of online (flipped) learning in PE (Killian et al., 2021, 2022; Østerlie & Bjerke, 2021). Using asynchronous online technology requires students to self-direct their learning which students may not be used to in PE, there is a learning and implementation curve for PE teachers, and school districts may lack important structures and policies to support student learning through technology. Nevertheless, there are practical theories and strategies available that support student acceptance and use of online (flipped) learning in PE, which are described in detail in chapters 7–9.

Extending physical activity opportunities with FL?

The ability of FL to *extend* physical activity opportunities within PE is somewhat limited according to how this mechanism is operationalized within the TEO. Using FL will not magically convince administrators to add 20 minutes onto the currently allotted 48-minute PE class periods at your school, for example. However, the approach does, in a way, extend PE *learning* opportunities for students using online content. Otherwise stated, the online component of FL offers teachers extra time to teach, prompt, encourage, and assess students, thereby effectively *extending* the amount of PE contact time they have with students. This occurs through the digital component, so this effectively equates to expansion. So, while the way in which FL can extend students' PE learning opportunities deviates slightly from how the TEO might define it, students in flipped PE classes still receive additional PE time through the online instruction than students who only attend face-to-face classes.

Research on the TEO and FL

So far, these potentials are largely anecdotal and based on practical observations. This is due to the limited amount of research conducted on this topic, to date. There have been peripheral findings that point to the potential of FL to *expand* PE opportunities (Sargent & Casey, 2020), as well as a growing base of evidence related to its abilities to *enhance* learning (Østerlie, 2020). Only one exploratory study has been implemented on FL in PE using the TEO (Killian et al., 2022). This study explored what happened when a class participated in a unit taught using FL and compared the observed outcomes to what happened during another class, which participated in the same unit taught only through direct instruction. Key findings indicated students receiving flipped instruction participated in additional physical activity during all lessons. There were also distinct differences in the amount of time students spent in skill practice and game play, with students in the flipped class engaging in more related opportunities. These results are supported by Campos-Gutiérrez et al. (2021) which also reported increased motor practice time for students participating in FL. Both studies indicate an enhancement effect for lessons/students participating in FL. In Killian et al's. (2022) study, variations in teacher involvement and lesson context offered insight into potential mechanisms responsible for enhanced physical activity during FL lessons. The teacher spent significantly less time in management and large group direct instruction tasks while teaching students in the flipped class and more time providing individual and small group instruction, however further research is necessary to confirm (or contradict) these results.

The FL approach offers a promising method for increasing active learning opportunities in PE to support students' progress toward meeting educational standards as well as their engagement in recommended daily physical activity. This can occur through the *expansion* of at-home physical activity and *enhancement* of face-to-face PE. It can also *extend* contact time to allow for more in-depth learning through asynchronous, on-demand video instruction.

Implications for whole school approaches to physical activity promotion

Whole-of-school approaches have gained acceptance in national and international recommendations associated with the promotion of youth physical activity engagement (Carson & Webster, 2019). One popular related framework is the CSPAP (Figure 4.2; Centers for Disease Control and Prevention [CDC], 2019).

The CSPAP framework represents the national model for PE in the United States and aspects of the CSPAP framework are apparent in similar multi-component youth physical activity approaches world-wide (Institute of Medicine [IOM], 2013; McMullen et al., 2015). The CSPAP framework shares similar goals with international whole-of-school approaches including ensuring all students receive quality PE, increasing practice opportunities for skills learned during PE, and helping students meet recommendations for daily physical activity (Society of Health and Physical Educators [SHAPE] America, 2015). With PE as its cornerstone, the purpose of a CSPAP is to operate by leveraging available assets to expand physical activity opportunities

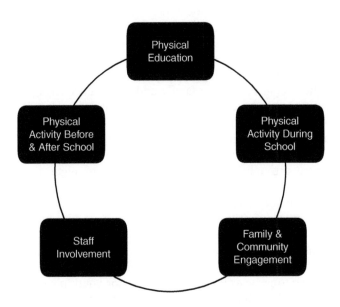

Figure 4.2 Comprehensive School Physical Activity Program Framework. Adapted from Centers for Disease Control and Prevention [CDC] (2019). This image was developed by the CDC and can be found free of charge on its website. Use of the image for this book does not imply endorsement of content by CDC, ATSDR, HHS or the United States Government of the authors, authors' institutions, Routledge, or this book.

for students beyond the PE context to before and after school, during school, and outside of school within the community.

Online PE is being recognized as an emerging asset that has potential to contribute to CSPAPs PE and public health goals (Webster et al., 2021) and the online, digital instruction embedded within FL approach represents one potential avenue for supporting CSPAP goals, particularly by engaging families and communities. Family and community engagement are essential to child development and physical activity engagement, which is why they represent a key component of whole-of-school physical activity promotion (Centers for Disease Control and Prevention [CDC], 2019; OECD, 2018). However, this component has been generally under researched aspect of CSPAPs, to date. Nevertheless, the asynchronous digital instruction format of FL offers a natural venue for PE teachers to promote family and community engagement in support of students' participation in instructional physical activity. This would occur through intentional prompting during the digital instruction and/or through the formative assessment process. In other words, teachers might think strategically to identify ways in which they can appropriately integrate opportunities for family and community engagement during their online FL instruction. For example, following video instruction and demonstrations, a teacher might encourage family and community engagement by prompting students to practice passing an object back and forth with someone in their family or household. Or they might prompt students to invite a family or household member to follow along during a basic dance sequence introduction or be a partner during a movement through imagery sequence. Teachers might also engage family and community in assessments by requiring students to teach a household member a skill using appropriate instructional cues or perform a creative movement sequence for an audience and reflect on the experience as a formative assessment.

The ways teachers can appropriately engage family and community through FL are only limited by the imagination. Whole-of-school approaches continue to grow as viable frameworks for youth physical activity promotion and the importance of the family and community to youth physical activity engagement is apparent. It seems natural for teachers to employ FL where appropriate to creatively expand physical activity opportunities and engage family and community.

The digital component of the FL format offers a natural way for teachers to expand and enhance learning and physical activity opportunities in PE, as well to support broader whole-of-school approaches to youth physical activity promotion. To do so requires intention, creativity, and support for students' (and family and community) participation of the digital and at-home aspect of their PE experience. Teachers can encourage expanded physical activity opportunities by going beyond passive instruction during their video instruction by integrating promotion of engagement in active learning at home. Using the digital component of FL strategically to preview upcoming in-class activities can also help teachers reduce their large group instruction time and student behaviour management, which allows students to engage in physical, applied learning more quickly thereby enhancing lesson quality. Teachers can invite families and household members into PE learning by suggesting at-home practice opportunities that can include multiple people and prompting students to encourage others to participate with them. Ultimately FL can support teachers in the provision of quality PE learning experiences in and out of school.

Questions for reflection

- What are the key tenants of the Theory of Expanded, Extended, and Enhanced Opportunities (TEO) for Youth Physical Activity Promotion?
- What are some ways that flipped learning can expand, extend, and enhance physical education learning opportunities?
- How might flipped learning support whole school approaches to physical activity promotion?
- What challenges might teachers encounter when using flipped learning to engage family and or household members through digital instruction?
- What are some barriers that might student engagement in at-home physical education engagement?

References

Alderman, B. L., Benham-Deal, T., Beighle, A., Erwin, H. E., & Olson, R. L. (2012). Physical education's contribution to daily physical activity among middle school youth. *Pediatric Exercise Science, 24*(4), 634–648.

Bailey, R. (2006). Physical education and sport in schools: A review of benefits and outcomes. *Journal of School Health, 76*(8), 397–401.

Beets, M. W., Okely, A., Weaver, R. G., Webster, C., Lubans, D., Brusseau, T., Carson, R., & Cliff, D. P. (2016). The theory of expanded, extended, and enhanced opportunities for youth physical activity promotion. *International Journal of Behavioral Nutrition and Physical Activity, 13*(1), 1–15. doi:10.1186/s12966-016-0442-2

Borgen, J. S., Hallås, B. O., Løndal, K., Mordal Moen, K., & Gjølme, E. G. (2020). Problems created by the (un)clear boundaries between physical education and physical activity health initiatives in schools. *Sport, Education and Society*, 1–14. doi:10.1080/13573322.2020.1722090

Campos-Gutiérrez, L. M., Sellés-Pérez, S., García-Jaén, M., & Ferriz-Valero, A. (2021). A flipped learning in physical education: Learning, motivation and motor practice time. *Revista Internacional de Medicina y Ciencias de la Actividad Fisica y del Deporte, 21*(81), 63–81. doi:10.15366/rimcafd2021.81.005

Carson, R., & Webster, C. A. (2019). *Comprehensive school physical activity programs: Putting evidence-based research into practice.* Human Kinetics.

Centers for Disease Control and Prevention [CDC]. (2019). *Increasing physical education and physical activity: A framework for schools.* US Department of Health and Human Services. https://www.cdc.gov/healthyschools/physicalactivity/pdf/2019_04_25_PE-PA-Framework_508tagged.pdf

Ennis, C. D. (2010). On their own: Preparing students for a lifetime. *Journal of Physical Education, Recreation & Dance, 81*(5), 17–22. doi:10.1080/07303084.2010.10598475

Ennis, C. D. (2011). Physical education curriculum priorities: Evidence for education and skillfulness. *Quest, 63*(1), 5–18. doi:10.1080/00336297.2011.10483659

Erwin, H., Beighle, A., Carson, R. L., & Castelli, D. M. (2013). Comprehensive school-based physical activity promotion: A review. *Quest, 65*(4), 412–428. doi:10.1080/00336297.2013.791872

Goad, T., Killian, C. M., & Daum, D. N. (2021). Distance learning in physical education: Hindsight is 2020 – part 3. *Journal of Physical Education, Recreation & Dance, 92*(4), 18–21. doi:10.1080/07303084.2021.1886843

Institute of Medicine [IOM]. (2013). *Educating the student body: Taking physical activity and physical education to school.* The National Academic Press.

Killian, C. M., Espinoza, S. M., Webster, C. A., Long, B., Urtel, M., Woods, A. M., & D'Agostino, E. (2022). Flipping the script: An initial exploration of flipped learning as an enhanced alternative to traditional physical education lessons. Manuscript submitted for publication.

Killian, C. M., Graber, K. C., & Woods, A. M. (2016). Flipped instructional model in physical education. In D. Novak, B. Antala, & D. Knjaz (Eds.), *Physical education and new technologies* (pp. 102–111). Croatian Kinesiology Association.

Killian, C. M., Kinder, C. J., & Woods, A. M. (2019). Online and blended instruction in K–12 physical education: A scoping review. *Kinesiology Review, 8*(2), 110–129. doi:10.1123/kr.2019-0003

Killian, C. M., Woods, A. M., Graber, K. C., & Temple, T. J. (2021). Factors associated with high school physical education teachers' adoption of a supplemental online instructional system (iPE). *Journal of Teaching in Physical Education, 40*, 136–145. doi:10.1123/jtpe.2019-0188

McMullen, J., Ni Chroinin, D., Tammelin, T., Pogorzelska, M., & Van Der Mars, H. (2015). International approaches to whole-of-school physical activity promotion. *Quest, 67*(4), 384–399. doi:10.1080/00336297.2015.1082920

Naul, R., & Scheuer, C. (2020). *Research on physical education and school sport in Europe.* Meyer & Meyer.

OECD. (2018). *The future of education and skills: Education 2030.* O. Publishing. doi:10.1787/9789264239555-en

Østerlie, O. (2020). *Flipped learning in physical education: A gateway to motivation and (deep) learning* [Doctoral thesis, Norwegian University of Science and Technology]. Trondheim. https://hdl.handle.net/11250/2649972

Østerlie, O., & Bjerke, Ø. (2021). Flipped learning in physical education teacher education – The student perspective. Manuscript submitted for publication.

Østerlie, O., Chad, K.M., Sargent, J., Garcia-Jaen, M., Garcia-Martinez, S., & Ferriz-Valero, A. (2021). Flipped learning in physical education: A scoping review. *Manuscript submitted for publication.*

Sargent, J., & Casey, A. (2020). Flipped learning, pedagogy and digital technology: Establishing consistent practice to optimise lesson time. *European Physical Education Review, 26,* 70–84. 10.1177/1356336X19826603

Society of Health and Physical Educators [SHAPE] America. (2015). *Comprehensive school physical activity programs: Helping all students log 60 minutes of physical activity each day* (Position statement). http://www.shapeamerica.org/advocacy/positionstatements/

Society of Health and Physical Educators [SHAPE] America. (2016). *SHAPE of the nation report: Status of physical education in the USA.* https://www.shapeamerica.org/advocacy/son/2016/upload/Shape-of-the-Nation-2016_web.pdf

Sun, P.-C., Tsai, R. J., Finger, G., Chen, Y.-Y., & Yeh, D. (2008). What drives a successful e-Learning? An empirical investigation of the critical factors influencing learner satisfaction. *Computers & Education, 50*(4), 1183–1202. doi:10.1016/j.compedu.2006.11.007

Trost, S., & van der Mars, H. (2009). Why we should not cut PE. *Educational Leadership, 67*(4), 60–65.

Webster, C. A., D'Agostino, E., Urtel, M., McMullen, J., Culp, B., Loiacono, C. A. E., & Killian, C. M. (2021). Physical education in the COVID era: Considerations for online program delivery using the comprehensive school physical activity program framework. *Journal of Teaching in Physical Education, 40*(2), 327–336. doi:10.1123/jtpe.2020-0182

World Health Organization [WHO]. (2020). *WHO 2020 guidelines on physical activity and sedentary behaviour.* https://apps.who.int/iris/bitstream/handle/10665/336656/9789240015128-eng.pdf

5 Flipped Learning and Learning

Learning in physical education

In this chapter, we argue that flipped learning (FL) supports learning in physical education (PE). FL seems to both lay ground for more cognitive learning, motor learning, and what we define as deep learning. First, we contextualise what learning in PE is before we explore the role of FL in student learning in PE.

Recently, PE has been recognised more as a subject of knowledge than observed some decades ago (Larsson, 2016), and 'physical education teachers are being held accountable for student learning in the same way as their classroom peers' (Ward, 2013, p. 431). Nevertheless, teachers and students have found it difficult to express what should be learned in PE (Siedentop, 2002; Tinning, 2002). This trend has resulted in, or might be a result of, a narrower approach to PE focusing on (sport-like) content more than learning of content as elaborated on in Chapter 2. This phenomenon is claimed to partly be a result of a PE teacher education that is 'not adequately preparing future PE teachers to promote healthy, active lifestyles and is not addressing previously identified issues in health-related teaching and learning' (Harris, 2014, p. 466).

Several studies conclude with a student view of PE as a break from other subjects and more non-educational than a subject of learning (Lyngstad et al., 2019; Woods et al., 2012). Earlier, research has focused much on the curriculum, content, and the teaching of PE (Kirk et al., 2006), and still today, the topic of learning in PE is under-researched (Quennerstedt et al., 2011, 2014). Scholars like Larsson and Redelius (2008) call on researchers to change focus from studying activities (e.g., how to teach specific sports or activities) to studying learning outcomes. This is grounded in the uncertainty about the subject's educational purpose. The educational benefits claimed for PE were reviewed by Bailey et al. (2009), and they found, unsurprisingly

DOI: 10.4324/9781003203377-6

perhaps, that there is suggestive evidence of a distinctive role for PE in the acquisition and development of children's movement skills and physical competence. They further argue that the role of PE in cognitive and academic developments is barely understood, resulting in a call for researchers to work with practitioners and policy makers to agree which claims for educational benefits can – and should – be supported and then tested through research. In line with this review, other scholars have found that learning cognitive knowledge does not predict any physical activity behaviours in PE, nor vice versa (Haslem et al., 2016; Shen et al., 2007). However, this prediction is, in later years, more disputed (Corbin, 2021). In this book, we still assume that PE is a place for activity yet too disconnected from the call for focus on learning. Further, Placek (1983) found that keeping students 'busy, happy and good' superseded all other learning outcomes in PE. This reality is still today reflected in PE in several countries (Larsson & Nyberg, 2017; Moen et al., 2018; Ward & Griggs, 2018).

Situated learning

Students learn together in PE. Most activities are based on cooperation, and how and what the students learn must be seen in a social context where students' learning depends on their peers' actions, attitudes, and support. Imagine practicing tennis where your learning partner only obstructs you, shows a bad attitude, and gives you no support. This learning environment will definitely affect your learning outcome in tennis and your motivation to continue practising tennis. Situated learning (Lave & Wenger, 1991) contributes to a growing body of research that explores the situated character of human learning and communication. The roots of situated learning lie in the work of activity theorists such as Vygotsky, and ideas proposed by Dewey, Piaget, and Gibson (Brown et al., 1989). Lave and Wenger (1991), with the theory of situated learning, focus on the relationship between learning and the social situations in which the learning occurs. Rather than asking what kinds of cognitive processes and conceptual structures are involved, they ask what kinds of social engagements provide the proper context for learning to take place. This shift in thinking about teaching and learning is embraced and applied to PE by scholars like Kirk and Macdonald (1998) and Rovegno (2006) as a constructivist perspective on learning. Constructivist approaches emphasise that learning is an active process in which the individual seeks out information in relation to the task at hand (Kirk & Macdonald, 1998). In concert with constructivist perspectives, situated perspectives consider it very important for researchers and teachers to understand how students learn in school settings by understanding how students' pre-existing knowledge facilitates and impedes learning (Rovegno, 2006).

The situated perspectives have illustrated the need to understand the multiple cultures of the learner, teacher, school, and society: how these impact learners, and how to plan a curriculum and teaching in PE that leads to 'robust, meaningful knowledge useful in multiple contexts' (Rovegno, 2006, p. 271). We argue that FL can provide opportunities for quality situated learning in PE. This on the other hand demands that the teacher takes a somewhat different role in this context to what we have seen in a more traditional PE setting.

The teacher's role in student learning in PE

With the integration of digital technology in modern society and education, the teacher's role changes (Selander, 2021). This is described by Arstorp (2019) as changing into a parallel learning environment where the teacher and the students simultaneously enhance their knowledge. Kavanagh et al. (2017) stated that the role of the educator changes from 'lecturer' to 'guide', and that not only requires that the teacher becomes a learner, but that we explicitly define learning as 'mutually constructed meaning' (Baxter Magolda, 2012, p. 17). This view can be recognised as a constructivist view on learning and a situated learning environment. Kavanagh et al. (2017) further state that FL is constructivist by its very definition as 'we require students to become actively involved in their learning rather than passively recipients of information. The focus is there for switched from the teacher to the learner ... ' (p. 17). Selander (2021) describes this view in a modified didactical (intended to instruct) triangle (Figure 5.1).

FL promotes something of a change in the relationship between the teacher and the students as both have more time to interact. The interactions between student-teachers and among students change due to the emphasis on student active and cooperative learning activities. This change is welcomed as having a positive influence on the quality of classroom interactions and student engagement as found in recent research (Havik & Westergård, 2019). In the 'design-oriented didactical triangle' (Figure 5.1), the teacher and the student are no longer placed in a typically hierarchical way, but this somehow changed role of the teacher does not imply that the teacher is a less important part of students' learning. On the contrary, the teacher is rather more important as they now can guide and support the student exactly where and when

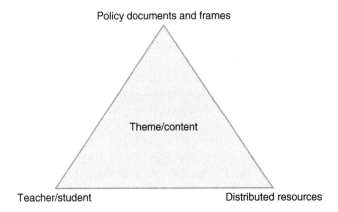

Policy documents and frames

Theme/content

Teacher/student   Distributed resources

Figure 5.1 The Design-Oriented Didactical Triangle. Adapted from 'Didaktiken efter Vygotskij: Design för lärande', by Selander (2021), freely translated from Swedish into English by the authors.

guidance and support are needed (Selander, 2021). Both students and teachers know that when digital tools are involved, the roles are likely to turn around, as the students often find them more competent than their teachers. An acknowledgement of this is important to further promote student competence as a resource in school, and this does not necessarily imply less quality in the education system.

Transforming PE to a subject of learning using FL

Students' learning in PE has been demonstrated to benefit from applying an FL framework (Ferriz-Valero et al., 2022; Hinojo et al., 2020; Østerlie & Kjelaas, 2019; Østerlie & Mehus, 2020). FL offers students the opportunity to see online videos resulting to be a beneficial use of a digital tool to enhance both cognitive, motor and skill learning. Hinojo et al. (2020) argue that FL is an effective teaching and learning methodology in both primary and secondary PE. They demonstrated that students' academic performance was significantly increased during an FL intervention, and that bettered interaction between teachers and students and between students was an important cause. Further, among secondary students, Østerlie and Mehus (2020) measured health-related fitness knowledge (HRFK), and Ferriz-Valero et al. (2022) measured conceptual knowledge in volleyball. Both studies found significantly better development among the intervention groups when compared to a control group (the group that did not receive the intervention). The videos used functioned as stimuli for preflection. Preflection is reflection-for-action as contrasted with reflection-in-action and reflection-on-action that guides future action based on past thoughts and actions (Wu et al., 2015). The students achieved a higher learning outcome as a function of preparing on the upcoming topics, prior to class. This assumption is supported by Jones and Bjelland (2004), as they stated that preflection 'adds an important component to developing core competencies and has the potential to further aid students in being able to reflect using higher order thinking responses and to generate knowledge' (pp. 963–964). Using video as a pre-class learning resource, the PE teacher can contribute to student learning in PE by informing specifically and thoroughly on what students are supposed to learn, as pointed out as being very important by Redelius et al. (2015). This form of pre-class content can also contribute to the teacher using problem-solving and guiding teacher strategies, as these approaches are pointed out by Larsson (2016) to promote student learning in PE. Through a constructivist lens, this preflection is important, as learning is an active process in which the individual seeks out information in relation to the task at hand (Kirk & Macdonald, 1998). In line with constructivist perspectives, the situated perspectives consider it very important for researchers and teachers to understand how students learn in school settings by understanding how students' pre-existing knowledge helps and hinders learning (Rovegno, 2006). Based upon these ideas, we argue that by its nature, FL facilitates and promotes learning in PE. It does this in three main ways in terms of enhancing a focus on learning, providing both more time and opportunities for learning, and promoting deeper learning through preflection.

As argued earlier, the traditional way of conducting PE does not include much focus on learning. We must move beyond what, e.g., Larsson and Redelius (2008) call, 'sweaty, smiley, and good kids' as the main objective of PE. The PE community must (even more) start talking about PE, conducting PE, and assessing student achievement in PE, with the mantra of PE being a subject of learning and competences. A change from the teacher showing proper technique, supposed to be conducted by all students, to a more exploratory approach to acquiring movement skills over time based on teachers reflecting on norms and values connected to different movement cultures is needed (Larsson, 2016). This is a shift away from a 'multi-activity-model', described by Kirk (2010) as a traditional, 'one-size-fits-all' technique-based model, to a more thematic-oriented curriculum model (Penney

& Chandler, 2000). This model is argued to promote student-centred teaching and facilitates creative roles and approaches to learning. The curriculum model is research-based, designed to clearly focus on the class content and cover several aims, and is thematic oriented, stretching over a longer timespan and encouraging a meaningful and holistic approach to PE (Lund & Tannehill, 2014).

The FL framework, as described in this book, seems to advocate more learning, as the individuals' learning is supported by peers and the teacher in a scaffolding fashion, also named cooperative learning or guided learning (Gillies & Boyle, 2005). The students seem to be assisted through the zone of proximal development (ZPD) as they are learning from student peers and a supportive teacher who has skills and knowledge beyond those of the learners. Fortunately, learning technologies can facilitate a change in both the process of teaching, learning, and assessing to a more student-centred and student-controlled learning environment, fostering autonomous motivated students (Collins & Halverson, 2018). It is a paradox that the highly autonomous aim of PE, upholding a lifelong, active, and healthy lifestyle, is reflected in so little autonomous focus in school PE, where teachers function as instructors and the students as conductors. If students are given more control of their learning, something that runs counter to the traditional learning exercised by schools, we can foster a generation of people who seek out learning. Involving the students in forming the class content, based on their experiences, is important for them to start seeing PE as something meaningful (Walseth et al., 2018). In other words, if we want the students to act autonomously, we need to prepare them for a physically active and healthy lifestyle in school by focusing on the students, focusing on their learning, and in a framework that enhances their autonomous and cooperative skills.

Kurban (2018) argues that students are looking for authentic learning experiences in their education that are useful for their life, requiring the FL approach in PE not only to include a flip of the instruction but also a transformation of class content and assessment to align with the students' 'real life'. Teachers must understand how students learn in school settings, which is upheld by Rovegno and Dolly (2006) as critically important in a situated perspective in concert with constructivist perspectives. As student leisure time has been digitalised, teachers must get insight into their 'real world' and apply this knowledge in practice in school. If the teacher, along with the student, as illustrated in Figure 5.1, gets this insight, explores, and learns *with* the students, this can lead to the development of what Rovegno (2006) calls 'robust, meaningful knowledge useful in multiple contexts' (p. 271). Robust, meaningful knowledge useful in multiple contexts is named, at least in the current political educational debate in Norway, as 'deep learning'.

FL and deep learning in PE

The question at this juncture is, how can FL support students' deep learning in PE? First, if there is uncertainty in what students are supposed to learn in PE, both among students and PE-teachers, how can researchers, teachers, or students recognise deep learning? Nevertheless, deep learning or transfer is suggested by Borgen and Hjardemaal (2017) to be operationalised and recognised as metacognition among students, stating that:

> The learner is considered an important and active part in his or her own learning. He or she is capable of setting realistic goals, and to examine thoughts, emotions and behaviour in such a manner that there is a reasonable probability of success.
>
> (p. 9)

This view of transfer is rooted in the work of Pellegrino and Hilton (2012) and Frey et al. (2016), who suggest that transfer is a possible result of deep learning. If a student learns something 'deep enough', this competence can be used to learn in other contexts or situations. Hence, transfer is happening. Birch et al. (2019) also support this view when suggesting that deep learning in PE can be recognised by students using competence from one situation to achieve new competence in another setting, for example, a student's skill in passing a basketball can help the student learn skills in passing a handball, or knowledge about training can transform into action from this student, resulting in better health. This view might be argued to be rooted in a 'cognitive' understanding of the concept of deep learning. This critique is supported by Dahl and Østern (2019), who present deep learning as a creating process, where body, relations, creative, affective, and cognitive processes *together* give depth to the learning as no part is unaffected by all the others.

Østerlie and Mehus (2020) and Ferriz-Valero et al. (2022) demonstrated that applying FL in PE gave a higher learning outcome regarding health-related fitness knowledge (HRFK) and conceptual knowledge in volleyball. The questions used in the tests were mostly of a kind recognised as surface learning, but also questions about how, e.g., the training of endurance is connected to one's own health were included. Considering the view of deep learning presented by Dahl and Østern (2019) and Tochon (2010), this could be recognised as deep learning, as the achievement demonstrated by the students on the tests were a combination of cognitive processes and participation in a relevant physical activity where the knowledge was 'experience'. This can be associated with what Tochon (2010) describes as 'meanings are embodied in action' (p. 6). Also, we must remember the statement of Frey et al. (2016) that deep learning is dependent on surface learning. From the results presented by Østerlie and Kjelaas (2019), we can draw several parallels to the presented assumptions. When an FL framework was applied, the students experienced learning more and deeper. They developed an understanding of how training affected health, and they experienced taking a more active part in their learning process as the online videos gave them a possibility to study and learn at their own pace and when they chose to do so. Through the students' statements, they found an experienced greater control of their own learning process, and this is (Kavanagh et al., 2017) the basis for constructivist learning. This promotion of self-paced learning resulted in higher motivation for preparing for, and engaging in, PE. As motivation is by Pellegrino and Hilton (2012) and Tochon (2010) stated to ground or mediate deep learning, further support for stating that FL supports deep learning in PE is found. Ennis (2015) suggested applying innovative approaches to PE in integrating PA with conceptual understanding, as the FL framework promotes, and stated that such 'knowledge-based, academic approaches to PE permit students to gain deep understandings that can be applied outside of PE across a range of physical activities in many different venues' (p. 123). Comparing the presented research with the statement by Ennis, a suggestion of deep learning being facilitated by FL is appropriate.

Through this chapter, we can conclude with the statement that FL seems to expand, extend, and enhance opportunities for learning in PE. This can be recognised as learning on various levels, from surface to deep.

Questions for reflection

- Do I think of PE as an arena for learning or activity (or both)? Why or why not?
- How would I define, and recognise, deep learning in PE students?
- How can I promote more and deeper learning in my PE students?
- How do I currently use situated learning in my practice?

References

Arstorp, A.-T. (2019). Hva er lærerens profesjonsfaglige digitale kompetanse? In T. A. Wølner, K. Kverndokken, M. Moe, & H. H. Siljan (Eds.), *101 digitale grep: En didaktikk for profesjonsfaglig digital kompetanse* (pp. 17–32). Fagbokforlaget.

Bailey, R., Armour, K., Kirk, D., Jess, M., Pickup, I., Sandford, R., Education, B. P., & Sport Pedagogy Special Interest Group. (2009). The educational benefits claimed for physical education and school sport: An academic review. *Research Papers in Education*, 24(1), 1–27. doi:10.1080/02 671520701809817

Baxter Magolda, M. B. (2012). Building learning partnerships. *Change: The Magazine of Higher Learning*, 44(1), 32–38. doi:10.1080/00091383.2012.636002

Birch, J., Vinje, E. E., Moser, T., & Skrede, J. (2019). Dybdelæring i kroppsøving: Utfordringer for kroppsøvingslæreren. In E. E. Vinje & J. Skrede (Eds.), *Fremtidens kroppsøvingslærer* (pp. 13–29). Cappelen Damm Akademisk.

Borgen, J. S., & Hjardemaal, F. R. (2017). From general transfer to deep learning as argument for practical aesthetic school subjects? *Nordic Journal of Studies in Educational Policy*, 1–12. doi:10.1080/20020317.2017.1352439

Brown, J. S., Collins, A., & Duguid, P. (1989). Situated cognition and the culture of learning. *Educational Researcher*, 18(1), 32–42.

Collins, A., & Halverson, R. (2018). *Rethinking education in the age of technology: The digital revolution and schooling in America*. Teachers College Press.

Corbin, C. B. (2021). Conceptual physical education: A course for the future. *Journal of Sport and Health Science*, 10(3), 308–322. doi:10.1016/j.jshs. 2020.10.004

Dahl, T., & Østern, T. P. (2019). Dybde//læring med overflate og dybde. In T. P. Østern, T. Dahl, A. Strømme, J. A. Petersen, A.-L. Østern, & S. Selander (Eds.), *Dybde//læring: En flerfaglig, relasjonell og skapende tilnærming* (pp. 39–56). Universitetsforlaget.

Ennis, C. D. (2015). Knowledge, transfer, and innovation in physical literacy curricula. *Journal of Sport and Health Science*, 4, 119–124. doi:10.1016/ j.jshs.2015.03.001

Ferriz-Valero, A., Østerlie, O., García-Martínez, S., & Baena-Morales, S. (2022). Flipped classroom: A good way for lower secondary physical education students to learn volleyball. *Education Sciences*, 12(1), 1–14. doi: 10.3390/educsci12010026

Frey, N., Fisher, D., & Hattie, J. (2016). Surface, deep, and transfer? Considering the role of content literacy instructional strategies. *Journal of Adolescent Adult Literacy*, 60(5), 567–575. doi:10.1002/jaal.576

Gillies, R. M., & Boyle, M. (2005). Teachers' scaffolding behaviours during cooperative learning. *Asia-Pacific Journal of Teacher Education*, 33(3), 243–259. doi:10.1080/13598660500286242

Harris, J. (2014). Physical education teacher education students' knowledge, perceptions and experiences of promoting healthy, active lifestyles in secondary schools. *Physical Education and Sport Pedagogy*, *19*(5), 466–480. doi:10.1080/17408989.2013.769506

Haslem, L., Wilkinson, C., Prusak, K. A., Christensen, W. F., & Pennington, T. (2016). Relationships between health-related fitness knowledge, perceived competence, self-determination, and physical activity behaviors of high school students. *Journal of Teaching in Physical Education*, *35*(1), 27–37. doi:10.1123/jtpe.2014-0095

Havik, T., & Westergård, E. (2019). Do teachers matter? Students' perceptions of classroom interactions and student engagement. *Scandinavian Journal of Educational Research*, 1–20. doi:10.1080/00313831.2019.1577754

Hinojo, F. L., López, J. B., Fuentes, A. C., Trujillo, J. M. T., & Pozo, S. S. (2020). Academic effects of the use of flipped learning in physical education. *International Journal of Environmental Research and Public Health*, *17*(1), 276. doi:10.3390/ijerph17010276

Jones, L. B., & Bjelland, D. (2004). International experiential learning in agriculture. Proceedings of the 20th Annual Conference, Association for International Agricultural and Extension Education (AIAEE), Dublin, Ireland.

Kavanagh, L., Reidsema, C., McCredden, J., & Smith, N. (2017). Design considerations. In C. Reidsema, L. Kavanagh, R. Hadgraft, & N. Smith (Eds.), *The flipped classroom: Practice and practices in higher education*. Springer. http://link.springer.com/book/10.1007/978-981-10-3413-8

Kirk, D. (2010). *Physical education futures*. Routledge.

Kirk, D., & Macdonald, D. (1998). Situated learning in physical education. *Journal of Teaching in Physical Education*, *17*(3), 376–387.

Kirk, D., Macdonald, D., & O'Sullivan, M. (2006). *The handbook of physical education*. Sage.

Kurban, C. F. (2018). Designing effective, contemporary assessment on a flipped educational sciences course. *Interactive Learning Environments*, 1–17. doi:10.1080/10494820.2018.1522650

Larsson, H. (2016). *Idrott och helsa: I går, i dag, i morgon*. Liber.

Larsson, H., & Nyberg, G. (2017). 'It doesn't matter how they move really, as long as they move.' Physical education teachers on developing their students' movement capabilities. *Physical Education and Sport Pedagogy*, *22*(2), 137–149. doi:10.1080/17408989.2016.1157573

Larsson, H., & Redelius, K. (2008). Swedish physical education research questioned: Current situation and future directions. *Physical Education and Sport Pedagogy*, *13*(4), 381–398. doi:10.1080/17408980802353354

Lave, J., & Wenger, E. (1991). *Situated learning: Legitimate peripheral participation*. Cambridge University Press.

Lund, J., & Tannehill, D. (2014). *Standards-based physical education curriculum development* (3rd ed.). Jones & Bartlett Publishers.

Lyngstad, I., Bjerke, Ø., & Lagestad, P. (2019). Students' views on the purpose of physical education in upper secondary school. Physical education as a break in everyday school life – learning or just fun? *Sport, Education and Society*, 1–12. doi:10.1080/13573322.2019.1573421

Moen, K. M., Westlie, K., Bjørke, L., & Brattli, V. H. (2018). *Physical education between ambition and tradition: National survey on physical education in primary school in Norway (Grade 5–10)*. https://brage.bibsys.no/xmlui/handle/11250/2482450

Østerlie, O., & Kjelaas, I. (2019). The perception of adolescents' encounter with a flipped learning intervention in Norwegian physical education. *Frontiers in Education, 4*(114), 1–12. doi:10.3389/feduc.2019.00114

Østerlie, O., & Mehus, I. (2020). The impact of flipped learning on cognitive knowledge learning and intrinsic motivation in Norwegian secondary physical education. *Education Sciences, 10*(110), 1–16. doi:10.3390/educsci10040110

Pellegrino, J. W., & Hilton, M. L. (2012). *Education for life and work: Developing transferable knowledge and skills in the 21st century*. The National Academies Press. http://nap.edu/13398

Penney, D., & Chandler, T. (2000). Physical education: What future(s)? *Sport, Education and Society, 5*(1), 71–87. doi:10.1080/135733200114442

Placek, J. (1983). Conceptions of success in teaching: Busy, happy and good. In T. J. Templin & J. Olson (Eds.), *Teaching in physical education* (pp. 46–56). Human Kinetics.

Quennerstedt, M., Annerstedt, C., Barker, D., Karlefors, I., Larsson, H., Redelius, K., & Öhman, M. (2014). What did they learn in school today? A method for exploring aspects of learning in physical education. *European Physical Education Review, 20*(2), 282–302. doi:10.1177/1356336X14524864

Quennerstedt, M., Öhman, J., & Öhman, M. (2011). Investigating learning in physical education: A transactional approach. *Sport, Education and Society, 16*(2), 159–177. doi:10.1080/13573322.2011.540423

Redelius, K., Quennerstedt, M., & Öhman, M. (2015). Communicating aims and learning goals in physical education: Part of a subject for learning? *Sport, Education and Society, 20*(5), 641–655. doi:10.1080/13573322.2014.987745

Rovegno, I. (2006). Situated perspectives on learning. In D. Kirk, D. MacDonald, & M. O'Sullivan (Eds.), *Handbook of physical education* (pp. 236–274). Sage.

Rovegno, I., & Dolly, J. P. (2006). Constructivist perspectives on learning. In D. Kirk, D. MacDonald, & M. O'Sullivan (Eds.), *Handbook of physical education* (pp. 242–261). Sage.

Selander, S. (2021). *Didaktiken efter Vygotskij: Design för lärande* (2nd ed.). Liber.

Shen, B., Chen, A., & Guan, J. (2007). Using achievement goals and interest to predict learning in physical education. *The Journal of Experimental Education, 75*(2), 89–108. doi:10.3200/JEXE.75.2.89-108

Siedentop, D. (2002). Content knowledge for physical education. *Journal of Teaching in Physical Education, 21*, 368–377.

Tinning, R. (2002). Engaging Siedentopian perspectives on content knowledge for physical education. *Journal of Teaching in Physical Education, 21*(4), 378–391.

Tochon, F. V. (2010). Deep education. *Journal for Educators, Teachers and Trainers, 1*, 1–12.

Walseth, K., Engebretsen, B., & Elvebakk, L. (2018). Meaningful experiences in PE for all students: An activist research approach. *Physical Education and Sport Pedagogy*, 1–15. doi:10.1080/17408989.2018.1429590

Ward, G., & Griggs, G. (2018). Primary physical education: A memetic perspective. *European Physical Education Review*, *24*(4), 400–417. doi:10.1177/1356336X16676451

Ward, P. (2013). The role of content knowledge in conceptions of teaching effectiveness in physical education. *Research Quarterly for Exercise and Sport*, *84*(4), 431–440. doi:10.1080/02701367.2013.844045

Woods, C. B., Tannehill, D., & Walsh, J. (2012). An examination of the relationship between enjoyment, physical education, physical activity and health in Irish adolescents. *Irish Educational Studies*, *31*(3), 263–280. doi:10.1080/03323315.2012.710068

Wu, L., Ye, X., & Looi, C.-K. (2015). Teachers' preflection in early stages of diffusion of an innovation. *Journal of Computers in Education*, *2*(1), 1–24. doi:10.1007/s40692-014-0022-x

6 Flipped Learning and Motivation

Motivation in physical education

As discussed in Chapter 2, one of the main aims of physical education (PE) globally is to motivate all students to engage in a lifelong physically active and a healthy lifestyle (Kirk, 2010) but unfortunately, 'many PE teachers report that motivating students is a significant challenge' (Bennie et al., 2016, p. 1), also during pandemic times (Dana et al., 2021). PE is one of the most popular subjects in school (Goodlad, 2004; Moen et al., 2018) but a major decline in motivation to participate in PE has been observed, especially among girls, as students move from primary to secondary and upper secondary school (Gao et al., 2008; Mowling et al., 2004; Prochaska et al., 2003; Säfvenbom et al., 2014; Xiang et al., 2004). Further, Goodlad (2004) observed that although PE is highly liked by students, it has the lowest perceived value among students, school administrators, and teaching staff. The decline in motivation is partly due to a 'sportified' PE favouring students, boys in particular, who conduct sports outside school (Andrews & Johansen, 2005; Dowling, 2016; Ennis, 1999; Green, 2008; Lundvall, 2016; Oliver & Kirk, 2015; Prochaska et al., 2003; Säfvenbom et al., 2014; Scraton, 2013; Vlieghe, 2013). This is also a topic mentioned in the second chapter of this book.

How can flipped learning be positive for student motivation in PE?

Two motivational theories are used in this chapter to shed light on how flipped learning (FL) can affect student motivation in PE. Both expectancy-value theory (EVT; Eccles, 1983; Eccles & Wigfield, 1995) and self-determination theory (SDT; Ryan & Deci, 2017) are broadly used as a theoretical framework when studying motivation in PE, and

DOI: 10.4324/9781003203377-7

in general are acknowledged as major theories of motivation (Weiner, 2010). EVT includes beliefs about one's competence in a given domain, hence representing a broader area than a specific task (Gao et al., 2008; Wigfield et al., 2009). This broader approach works well with the PE subject, acquiring a wide competence involving both students' cognitive knowledge, physical and social competence. SDT was chosen, as this theory is one of the few motivational theories that focus on the role of choice and autonomy in human behaviour. As PE often is a mandatory school subject, this is an important perspective to consider. Different from other theoretical frameworks, SDT recognises the controlling nature of schools and suggests the use of strategies consistent with this nature to encourage the fundamental human needs for autonomy, competence, and relatedness as motivation mediators (Sun & Chen, 2010).

While theory is often seen as irrelevant to practice, the approach taken in this chapter is one of viewing theory as a form of practice, with the two being inseparable. Both SDT and EVT provide the foundation for thoughts and tools for understanding and developing PE, and PE on the other hand has played a major role in forming and understanding student motivation by those same theories. Further, the nature of the FL framework, shifting from a teacher-centred to a more student-centred style, where the students are more actively involved in their learning processes, encourages students to act more autonomously. This chapter considers motivation in PE as a state more than a trait, a view supported by Reeve (2016), who argues that 'motivation is always a state' (p. 32). A motivational state is more likely to be formed, mediated, or changed by new experiences, while a motivational trait has no way of activating itself (Reeve, 2016). This assumption also imply that we in this chapter do not first seek to understand change in motivation over time, but we first and foremost seek to discover the underlying mechanisms which drive these changes: in other words, not only *how* but equally important *why* motivation in PE acts when FL is applied.

There are several studies looking into how the implementation of FL in PE can affect student motivation. Distinctions in how these studies have looked at motivation lead us to explore the result both considering gender, context, and autonomy. In general, implementation of an FL framework seems to halt the observed decline, or even result in increases, in student motivation in PE. In an EVT perspective, expectancy beliefs (EB), which Zhu et al. (2012) refer to as one's broad beliefs about one's competence in a given domain, was shown by Østerlie (2018b) to increase among girls. Attainment value (AV), which Eccles and Wigfield (2002) refer to as a person's perceived importance of doing well on a task, was shown in Østerlie (2018b) to increase among girls. Motivational cost, which Wigfield (1994) refers to as the negative aspects of engaging in a task, such as the fear of failure or lost opportunities due to choosing one task over another, was demonstrated by Østerlie (2018a) to change in a positive direction among girls. In an SDT perspective, intrinsic motivation (IM), which Deci and Ryan (1985) suggest exists when individuals participate because of an inherent enjoyment or interest in the activity, was shown by Østerlie and Mehus (2020) not to decrease among the boys as happened among the boys in the control group (i.e., the group of students not experiencing FL). Using the same theoretical lens, Ferriz-Valero et al. (2022) found all students to motivationally benefit from FL, while Campos-Gutiérrez et al. (2021) found no change in motivation when comparing to a control group. Østerlie and Kjelaas (2019) demonstrated a positive perception of FL in PE by students, both boys and girls, who reported a positive attitude towards preparing prior to class, a rise in motivation due to an increased valuation of PE, and a perceived positive effect on understanding and learning in PE.

When combined, this represents some empirical evidence for the assumptions that FL positively influences motivation among PE students. There now follows a discussion on the positive impact FL seems to have on student motivation to participate in PE considering gender, contextualisation, and autonomy.

Does FL motivate all students?

We suggest that FL is an approach that benefits a variety of students, either regarding PA levels, gender, level of motivation, or interest for PE. Some evidence shows that girls find FL to re-define PE not as a 'boys' subject' as their EB, AV, and perceived cost of attending are observed to change in a positive direction (Østerlie, 2018a, 2018b). One reason why FL in PE seems to benefit girls more than boys regarding motivation can be found in the fact that PE traditionally is more beneficial for boys than for girls. This is shown to apply in many countries (Kirk, 2010; Säfvenbom et al., 2014). Hence, boys may not welcome a change to the subject as much as girls might do. On the other hand, a change should be welcomed by both students, PE teachers, school leaders, and policy makers, as girls are shown to have a lower motivation for PE, and their performance in PE (measured by their final grade in compulsory schooling) is, in several countries, lower compared to that of boys. If girls perform less well, they might be inclined to take more advantage of the offered resources to reduce the observed and experienced gap. This assumption is supported by Chiang et al. (2018), who found female college students in Taiwan took more advantage of the FL approach compared to male students, who preferred a traditional approach when applying an FL framework in PE basketball. Further, if PE traditionally benefits boys, the expectancy for success would naturally be lower among girls compared to boys. This was demonstrated in studies by Zhu et al. (2012) and Gao (2009), who demonstrated that girls have a lover EB than boys in primary and middle school. Nevertheless, there are arguments that boys find that FL helps them to contextualise the activities, resulting in stabilising their IM for PE (Østerlie & Mehus, 2020), and as mentioned earlier, some studies do not find differences in gender regarding how FL affects student motivation in PE. The way FL has been applied, in general across the earlier mentioned studies, encouraged more co-operation and facilitated more interactions between both teacher and students, and among students. Havik and Westergård (2019) have suggested that emotional support from the teacher and perceived high-quality classroom interactions have a strong association with student engagement. Taking an overview so far, we can see that FL seems to affect student motivation in PE in different ways depending on the context, type of intervention, and who the students are. So far, the literature on the topic is too scarce to make firm conclusions, but we can suggest that all students seem to benefit from FL regarding their motivation for participation and learning in PE.

Motivation through context

It is suggested that PE students feel the importance of understanding why they do the activities in class; they need a context (Østerlie, 2020). A similar argument has been expressed by Bennie et al. (2016) regarding Australian PE teachers implementing different strategies to enhance student motivation, PA, and learning. The teachers reported 'the "explaining relevance" strategy to be the most effective and acceptable strategy for increasing student enjoyment, motivation, PA, and learning during PE lessons' (p. 9) followed by the strategy of 'giving choice'.

The approach of *how* to contextualise the activities in PE deserves attention. For the student to understand the context they need to be informed of that context, and the implementation of a digital tool like online videos seemed to be a positive contribution to this matter. How this contextualisation (the process of understanding and becoming familiar with the context) can look like is further described through some cases presented in Chapter 9. Contextualisation seems to help students to be assisted through the space between what a learner can do without assistance and what a learner can do with adult guidance or in collaboration with more capable peers, defined as the Zone of Proximal Development (ZPD). This process is described by Sun and Chen (2010) as 'an individual's ZPD is satisfied through internalizing knowledge acquired through communicating with the others' (Sun & Chen, 2010, pp. 370–371). Nevertheless, how PE education is delivered where one wants to incorporate both cognitive and physical features in the learning process as a too vigorous context might shift student motivation away from cognitive learning towards physical participation (Chen et al., 2013).

To understand why students seem to differ in their needs of contextualisation when there is a change in the practical content, one must also take account of the constructivist view. The constructivist approach, suggested by Kirk and Macdonald (1998), argues that learning is an active process in which the individual seeks out information in relation to the task at hand. It seems that some students welcomed the change more than others; thus, the importance of seeking out information related to the activities in class seemed more important to some than others when motivation was related to the activities per se. When the information concerned practical information like the type of activity and the intensity of the activity, Østerlie and Kjelaas (2019) and Ferriz-Valero et al. (2022) suggest that this type of contextualisation is important for all students. In sum, it seems to be important for student motivation in PE to include both physical activity and cognitive learning to provide a context, and FL seems to facilitate and promote this.

Motivation through autonomy

Østerlie and Mehus (2020) and Ferriz-Valero et al. (2022) suggest that students' IM was affected positively by FL when compared to a control group. IM contributes to what is called autonomous motivation in an SDT perspective. As students are informed on class content and are then able to contextualise the activities with cognitive knowledge, they seem to enhance their autonomy regarding their learning process. This assumption finds parallels to Chapter 4, where autonomy seems to be important for physical activity outside school as well. Østerlie and Kjelaas (2019) further suggested that students appreciated FL as a mean of acquiring more control over their learning situations in PE as they could choose to engage in the preflection materials: the online videos assigned as homework, and in this way control the pace of their learning process. Through this we can see that the videos function as part of the scaffold, what Yelland and Masters (2007) call technical scaffolding, supporting student learning in PE. As students become more self-driven and take more control of their learning, supported by a scaffold that consists of the teacher, peer students, and technology prompts, their autonomous motivation rises, and their learning outcome improves. This suggestion is supported by Ntoumanis and Standage (2009), who concluded that if the PE teacher provided a meaningful rationale, expressing the importance of par- taking in that activity (e.g., health benefits), inherent interest in PE was supported. The assumption of the students included in the present project becoming more self-driven is further supported by Bing (2017), who found an obvious increase in students' self-study ability after applying FL in university PE, and by Ryan and Deci (2017), who linked a rise in autonomous motivation to a rise in engagement.

The teacher, working in the role of supporter and guide in the students' learning process, provides more possibilities for in- dividualisation and tailor-made support. This assumption is further supported by Lekanger and Olsen (2019), who state that the use of digital technology in school makes it easier for the teacher to see each student's possibilities and needs, and support adapting the education to each individual. They further suggest that technology can be a positive enhancer for learning focus in class and a facilitator for each student's learning, and this is important when considering adapted education. The conflict between autonomy development and the controlling nature of schooling serves as an example reminding us of the need to re-examine the way we conduct PE.

The nature of an FL learning environment produces more oppor- tunities to give the students choices. Bennie et al. (2016) and Lonsdale et al. (2009) found that giving students opportunities to make choices in PE was a successful strategy to enhance student motivation, PA levels, and student learning. In an FL context, the preparation mate- rial can contain an introduction to a variety of activities, or a set of videos, from which the students can select. In this way, students can choose to engage in different activities in class, and the teacher is not bound to instruct a whole class that subsequently often does the same activity. This, on the other hand, requires a change in how PE is conducted today, as the subject and its content is activity driven (Dyson, 2014; Ennis, 2011), and not objective driven, with minimal room for individualisation. PE teachers must support students in deciding on their individual objectives, based in the curriculum aims, and realise that there might be a variety of ways to achieve these objectives. In sum, FL seems to enhance students' sense of autonomy in PE, resulting in a positive impact on their autonomous motivation for both preparing for and participating in PE.

In light of both EVT and SDT, we can conclude that FL seems to affect student motivation in PE in various ways, and on different levels supporting motivation for both low-motivated students and high-motivated students.

Questions for reflection

- How do I consider the current motivation(s) for PE among my students?
- How can an FL approach affect this motivation?
- How can I design my FL classes so that all students are motivated for participation?
- How can I, through my role as teacher in PE, support autonomy in students when applying FL?

References

Andrews, T., & Johansen, V. (2005). Gym er det faget jeg hater mest. *Norsk Pedagogisk Tidsskrift, 89*(04), 302–314.

Bennie, A., Peralta, L., Gibbons, S., Lubans, D., & Rosenkranz, R. (2016). Physical education teachers' perceptions about the effectiveness and acceptability of strategies used to increase relevance and choice for students in physical education classes. *Asia-Pacific Journal of Teacher Education*, 1–18. doi:10.1080/1359866X.2016.1207059

Bing, Z. (2017). A survey analysis of the network flipped classroom model application in the optimization of the university physical education classroom system. *Boletín Técnico, 55*(19), 413–418.

Campos-Gutiérrez, L. M., Sellés-Pérez, S., García-Jaén, M., & Ferriz-Valero, A. (2021). A flipped learning in physical education: Learning, motivation and motor practice time. *Revista Internacional de Medicina y Ciencias de la Actividad Física y del Deporte, 21*(81), 63–81. doi:10.15366/rimcafd2021.81.005

Chen, S., Chen, A., Sun, H., & Zhu, X. (2013). Physical activity and fitness knowledge learning in physical education: Seeking a common ground. *European Physical Education Review, 19*(2), 256–270. doi:10.1177/1356336X13486058

Chiang, T. H.-C., Yang, S. J., & Yin, C. (2018). Effect of gender differences on 3-on-3 basketball games taught in a mobile flipped classroom. *Interactive Learning Environments*, *27*(8), 1093–1105. doi:10.1080/10494820.2018.1495652

Dana, A., Khajehaflaton, S., Salehian, M. H., & Sarvari, S. (2021). Effects of an intervention in online physical education classes on motivation, intention, and physical activity of adolescents during the COVID-19 pandemic. *International Journal of School Health*, *8*(3), 158–166. doi:10.30476/intjsh.2021.91103.1145

Deci, E. L., & Ryan, R. M. (1985). *Intrinsic motivation and self-determination in human behavior*. Plenum.

Dowling, F. (2016). De idrettsflinkes arena: Ungdoms fortellinger fra kroppsøvingsfaget med blikk på sosial klasse. In Ø. Seippel, M. K. Sisjord, & Å. Strandbu (Eds.), *Ungdom og Idrett* (pp. 249–268). Cappelen Damm akademisk.

Dyson, B. (2014). Quality physical education: A commentary on effective physical education teaching. *Research Quarterly for Exercise and Sport*, *85*(2), 144–152. doi:10.1080/02701367.2014.904155

Eccles, J. S. (1983). Expectancies, values, and academic behaviors. In J. T. Spence (Ed.), *Achievement and achievement motives: Psychological and sociological approaches* (pp. 70–146). Freeman.

Eccles, J. S., & Wigfield, A. (1995). In the mind of the actor: The structure of adolescent achievement task values and expectancy-related beliefs. *Personality and Social Psychology Bulletin*, *21*(3), 215–225.

Eccles, J. S., & Wigfield, A. (2002). Motivational beliefs, values, and goals. *Annual Review of Psychology*, *53*, 109–132.

Ennis, C. D. (1999). Creating a culturally relevant curriculum for disengaged girls. *Sport, Education and Society*, *4*(1), 31–49. doi:10.1080/1357332990040103

Ennis, C. D. (2011). Physical education curriculum priorities: Evidence for education and skillfulness. *Quest*, *63*(1), 5–18. doi:10.1080/00336297.2011.10483659

Ferriz-Valero, A., Østerlie, O., García-Martínez, S., & Baena-Morales, S. (2022). Flipped classroom: A good way for lower secondary physical education students to learn volleyball. *Education Sciences*, *12*(1), 1–14. doi:10.3390/educsci12010026

Gao, Z. (2009). Students' motivation, engagement, satisfaction, and cardiorespiratory fitness in physical education. *Journal of Applied Sport Psychology*, *21*, S102–S115. doi:10.1080/10413200802582789

Gao, Z., Lee, A. M., & Harrison, L. Jr. (2008). Understanding students' motivation in sport and physical education: From the expectancy-value model and self-efficacy theory perspectives. *Quest*, *60*(2), 236–254. doi:10.1080/00336297.2008.10483579

Goodlad, J. I. (2004). *A place called school: Twentieth anniversary edition* (2nd ed.). McGraw-Hill.

Green, K. (2008). *Understanding physical education.* Sage.

Havik, T., & Westergård, E. (2019). Do teachers matter? Students' perceptions of classroom interactions and student engagement. *Scandinavian Journal of Educational Research,* 1–20. doi:10.1080/00313831.2019.1577754

Kirk, D. (2010). *Physical education futures.* Routledge.

Kirk, D., & Macdonald, D. (1998). Situated learning in physical education. *Journal of Teaching in Physical Education, 17*(3), 376–387.

Lekanger, T., & Olsen, M. H. (2019). Teknolog for å fremme et positivt læringsmiljø. In T. Lekanger & M. H. Olsen (Eds.), *Teknologi og læringsmiljø* (pp. 49–65). Universittsforlget.

Lonsdale, C., Sabiston, C. M., Raedeke, T. D., Ha, A. S. C., & Sum, R. K. W. (2009). Self-determined motivation and students' physical activity during structured physical education lessons and free choice periods. *Preventive Medicine, 48,* 69–73. doi:10.1016/j.ypmed.2008.09.013

Lundvall, S. (2016). Approaching a gender neutral PE-culture? An exploration of the phase of a divergent PE-culture. *Sport in Society, 19*(5), 640–652. doi:10.1080/17430437.2015.1073944

Moen, K. M., Westlie, K., Bjørke, L., & Brattli, V. H. (2018). *Physical education between ambition and tradition: National survey on physical education in primary school in Norway (Grade 5–10).* https://brage.bibsys.no/xmlui/handle/11250/2482450

Mowling, C. M., Brock, S. J., Eiler, K. K., & Rudisill, M. (2004). Student motivation in physical education breaking down barriers. *Journal of Physical Education, Recreation & Dance, 75*(6), 40–45. doi:10.1080/07303084.2004.10607256

Ntoumanis, N., & Standage, M. (2009). Motivation in physical education classes: A self-determination theory perspective. *School Field, 7*(2), 194–202. doi:10.1177/1477878509104324

Oliver, K. L., & Kirk, D. (2015). *Girls, gender and physical education: An activist approach.* Routledge.

Østerlie, O. (2018a). Adolescents' perceived cost of attending physical education: A flipped learning intervention. *Journal for Research in Arts and Sports Education, 2*(3), 1–17. doi:10.23865/jased.v4.1197

Østerlie, O. (2018b). Can flipped learning enhance adolescents' motivation in physical education? An intervention study. *Journal for Research in Arts and Sports Education, 2,* 1–15. doi:10.23865/jased.v2.916

Østerlie, O. (2020). *Flipped learning in physical education: A gateway to motivation and (deep) learning* [Doctoral thesis, Norwegian University of Science and Technology]. Trondheim. https://hdl.handle.net/11250/2649972

Østerlie, O., & Kjelaas, I. (2019). The perception of adolescents' encounter with a flipped learning intervention in Norwegian physical education. *Frontiers in Education, 4*(114), 1–12. doi:10.3389/feduc.2019.00114

Østerlie, O., & Mehus, I. (2020). The impact of flipped learning on cognitive knowledge learning and intrinsic motivation in Norwegian secondary physical education. *Education Sciences, 10*(110), 1–16. doi:10.3390/educsci10040110

Prochaska, J. J., Sallis, J. F., Slymen, D. J., & McKenzie, T. L. (2003). A longitudinal study of children's enjoyment of physical education. *Pediatric Exercise Science, 15*, 170–178.

Reeve, J. (2016). A grand theory of motivation: Why not? *Motivation and Emotion, 40*(1), 31–35. doi:10.1007/s11031-015-9538-2

Ryan, R. M., & Deci, E. L. (2017). *Self-determination theory: Basic psychological needs in motivation, development, and wellness.* The Guilford Press.

Säfvenbom, R., Haugen, T., & Bulie, M. (2014). Attitudes toward and motivation for PE: Who collects the benefits of the subject? *Physical Education and Sport Pedagogy, 20*(6), 629–646. doi:10.1080/17408989.2014.892063

Scraton, S. (2013). Feminism and physical education: Does gender still matter. In G. Pfister & M. K. Sisjord (Eds.), *Gender and sport: Changes and challenges* (pp. 199–216). Waxmann Verlag.

Sun, H., & Chen, A. (2010). A pedagogical understanding of the self-determination theory in physical education. *Quest, 62*(4), 364–384. doi:10.1080/00336297.2010.10483655

Vlieghe, J. (2013). Physical education beyond sportification and biopolitics: An untimely defense of Swedish gymnastics. *Sport, Education and Society, 18*(3), 277–291. doi:10.1080/13573322.2011.566602

Weiner, B. (2010). The development of an attribution-based theory of motivation: A history of ideas. *Educational Psychologist, 45*(1), 28–36. doi:10.1080/00461520903433596

Wigfield, A. (1994). Expectancy-value theory of achievement motivation: A developmental perspective. *Educational Psychology Review, 6*(1), 49–78. doi:10.1007/bf02209024

Wigfield, A., Tonks, S., & Klauda, S. L. (2009). Expectancy-value theory. In K. R. Wentzel & A. Wigfield (Eds.), *Handbook of motivation at school* (pp. 55–75). Routledge.

Xiang, P., McBride, R., & Guan, J. (2004). Children's motivation in elementary physical education: A longitudinal study. *Research Quarterly for Exercise and Sport, 75*, 71–80. doi:10.1080/02701367.2004.10609135

Yelland, N., & Masters, J. (2007). Rethinking scaffolding in the information age. *Computers & Education, 48*, 362–382. doi:10.1016/j.compedu.2005.01.010

Zhu, X., Sun, H., Chen, A., & Ennis, C. (2012). Measurement invariance of expectancy-value questionnaire in physical education. *Measurement in Physical Education and Exercise Science, 16*(1), 41–54. doi:10.1080/10913 67X.2012.639629

Part II

Applications of Flipped Learning in Physical Education

7 When Flipped Learning Ambition Meets Physical Education Tradition

From theory and ambitions to practice

Building on the definitions and theoretical aspects of flipped learning (FL) identified in chapter 3, this chapter seeks to explore how these theories are applied in practice and seeks to question some of the practical considerations that you might have. Of course, it is quite tricky to pre-empt all of the considerations or aspects you might encounter in practice, but this chapter will seek to address some of the common aspects we know of from the literature or areas we have reflected on in helping to author this book.

Before we look at the context of physical education (PE), a useful starting point in considering FL is its application in a broader educational setting. Indeed, learning from different subjects, contexts, and applications gives us important aspects to consider for the subject of PE. In the context of chemistry, for example, a common method of applying FL is where students watch a pre-lecture screencast or video (averaging between 10 and 20 minutes), which in some cases is supplemented by handouts or reading (Seery, 2015). In engineering, despite the many benefits of FL identified such as flexibility, improved interaction, and engagement, there were also challenges reported such as increased workload, student resistance, and technical issues (Karabulut-Ilgu et al., 2018). There are many other examples of research reviews which you may wish to explore to get a general perspective of the approach (Birgili et al., 2021; Hew & Lo, 2018).

Given the greater presence of using FL in higher education and the limited research in relation to PE, we explore some of the lessons to be learnt from this context. Brewer and Movahedazarhouligh (2018) discuss how shifting to an FL model or approach can be an overwhelming task. Determining how, how much, and what to 'flip' is a critical decision (Brewer & Movahedazarhouligh, 2018). Drawing

DOI: 10.4324/9781003203377-9

upon the work of Fairbairn (2009) they discuss how there are four distinct and cyclic phases that occur when one transition to using FL.

1   Motivation to change
2   Preparations to flip
3   Adoption of pedagogy
4   Reflections on the benefits and challenges of adoption

We discuss each of these aspects in turn to consider FL in the context of PE.

Motivation to change

By this stage of the book, you may be thinking that this aspect is already complete. Indeed, you were motivated in some capacity (whether that is interest or opportunity) to buy or read this book and so you may already have the motivation to change or adapt your current practices in adopting FL. When we look back at the aspects of motivation covered in chapter 6 in relation to our own practice, you may have intrinsic motivation to try out a novel approach, you are developing contextualisation and autonomy, or you are motivated by the possible outcomes FL might be able to help your students to achieve that we have covered in the previous chapters.

We know from the current literature that aspects such as attitude are central to behavioural intentions and usage behaviours regarding technology (Dwivedi et al., 2019). We think that the same would apply to the use of technology embedded within FL in terms of considering your own attitudes regarding the approach and technology (see also chapter 6 which covers motivation).

Preparations to flip

At this stage, preparations to use FL may include:

*   Considering what aspects of support you might need such as that of parents, other teachers, and your school.
*   What technologies in terms of recording or delivering video content might you need?
*   Explaining the process to students, faculty, and administrators so that understanding and expectations can be clarified.
*   Alternative activities (e.g., providing a video on a memory stick or providing a video transcript for students to read) that could be

adopted if a student cannot access the internet or there is a problem with internet connections at home.

- Ensuring that the students have the prior knowledge or support needed to complete the learning at home.
- How your use of FL will fit into your own and others' ambitions for the year in terms of the curriculum and students' learning outcomes.

In considering this stage, it is worth reflecting on what content you will 'flip'. Considering what content and aspects of the curriculum could be learnt independently or that you require students to develop a better cognitive understanding is a useful starting point. As Østerlie (2016, p. 171) discusses by drawing upon the Norwegian PE curriculum, aspects such as 'explaining why physical activity is important in everyday life' is an example of an aspect of the curriculum that could be developed as home learning content.

The choice of whether to create your own videos or draw upon existing content is also a key phase when preparing to use FL. Bergmann and Sams (2012) recommend creating or using content that is no more than 15, and preferably less than 10 minutes in length. This is to ensure that there is a balance between the different activities (e.g., watching a video and completing a task as an example). Subsequently, as Østerlie (2016) explains, thinking about *what* content can be covered in this timeframe and considering whether a series of videos would work better than one lengthy video is important. We are conscious to point out here that this may indeed take a bit of trial and error to find out what content and how the structure of the content best works for the type of learning you are seeking to build on.

At this stage, thinking about how you will create your videos, how long it will take to create them and where you are going to put your videos so that students can access them cannot be overlooked (Østerlie, 2016). Bergmann and Sams (2012) claim that it may take up to three times more than the length of the video to create (i.e., a 10-minute video taking 30 minutes to produce). So, carving out time to write a script, consider your delivery, shooting your video (including perhaps several takes!) and editing it is time that you need to factor into your planning.

Østerlie (2016) explains how there are different pieces of software or platforms that you may want to use to record your videos. These range from screencasting software such as 'Camtasia' or free pieces of online software such as 'screencast-o-matic' that can be used to record what is displaying on your computer screen. Similarly, you can use other devices such as video cameras, webcams, mobile phones, or tablets to record. It is important to use what you have access to rather than trying to use pieces of technology or software that you may not be familiar with.

In relation to *where* you upload your videos for students to access, it may be possible for you to use your school's virtual learning environment (VLE) or different apps that your school has a licence for and uses across the curriculum. Alternatively, it may be more suitable for you to create a YouTube channel, share Google Drive, or create a DVD that students can watch at home. To reiterate Østerlie's (2016) reflections, it is all about finding a platform that is most suitable for you in terms of what access you have at your disposal and what fits your students' needs.

Adoption of pedagogy

This is the stage in which you will be implementing the aspects outlined in chapter 3 onwards with your students. With reference to the four pillars detailed in Flipped Learning Network [FLN] (2014), we detail the various stages, including reflective questions for you to consider.

Flexible environment

This could include adapting the physical environment but also the online environments you are using to deliver and distribute content. For some of your students, the environments you propose to support and guide their learning may be something they are unfamiliar with or have alternative preferences. Consider the end goals that you want students to achieve and whether the environment supports them in being able to get there.

Flexibility in this sense also relates to when students learn in terms of their learning timeline and how these dovetails with your assessment of their learning. For example, a student may need to watch a video and complete an activity at home before they can complete the assessment areas.

The below reflective questions are taken directly from the Flipped Learning Network [FLN] (2014, p. 2).

"I establish spaces and time frames that permit students to interact and reflect on their learning as needed".

"I continually observe and monitor students to make adjustments as appropriate".

"I provide students with different ways to learn content and demonstrate mastery".

These are currently written as 'reflective checkpoints' *after* your use of FL. Yet, breaking the different elements down to consider prior to your use (and in the planning stages) will also be of use. For example, you could consider:

- What spaces/timeframes have, or will you be establishing that allow students to interact and reflect on their learning? (e.g., VLE spaces, forums, chats, asynchronous or synchronous sessions)
- How will you observe or monitor students learning overtime to enable you to adjust? (e.g., having formative assessment points or small tasks for students to complete)
- In what ways will I provide students with different ways to learn content and demonstrate proficiency? (e.g., providing a video with audio and visual cues for students, supplementary reading, etc.)

Learning culture

When adopting FL, instruction is situated within a learner-centred approach. As such, learners are actively involved in knowledge construction as well as seeking to evaluate their own and even others' learning (e.g., peer support or group tasks). Supporting students to participate in and find learning approaches that are personally meaningful and recognisable to them will support the approach for both you and your students (Lynch & Sargent, 2020). As we learnt in chapter 2, the notion of homework is not necessarily 'the norm' for students in PE. Therefore, developing the understanding and learning culture behind the home-based activities ensures that students 'buy in' to the process.

"I give students opportunities to engage in meaningful activities without the teacher being central".

"I scaffold these activities and make them accessible to all students through differentiation and feedback".
(Flipped Learning Network [FLN], 2014, p. 2)

Consider how you ensure that activities are meaningful and that students can find meaning within their activities (e.g., Fletcher et al. (2021) argue that meaningful activities provide various aspects of meaning such as fun, delight, motor competence, challenge, or social interaction). What and how will you scaffold the activities to make the learning accessible to the students? What and how will you differentiate and when/how will feedback be provided? Be prepared that some of the aspects that you may plan for may need to be adapted for your students.

Intentional content

Simply giving students homework is not FL. Thinking about the content you can create or direct students towards that will intentionally support what they are trying to learn when they are at home on their own is paramount. They are very unlikely to have your immediate support and so considering the different abilities and levels of your students when creating this content allows you to think about the different pathways and aspects for differentiation that you can use to scaffold the learning materials. Some content may require independent learning whereas others might involve students collaborating or working in teams.

> "I prioritize concepts used in direct instruction for learners to access on their own".

> "I create and/or curate relevant content (typically videos) for my students".

> "I differentiate to make content accessible and relevant to all students".
>
> (Flipped Learning Network [FLN], 2014, p. 2)

With these statements in mind, what content will be relevant for students to work their way through independently? Where might the key problem areas be that students may not be able to progress through and what prompts or support could you provide to enable them to be supported? What pre-existing content could you draw upon and what gaps might you have to fill through creating your own content?

Professional educator

Observing students' progress, providing assessment and feedback, and ensuring that students have the elements they need to make their independent learning at home a success, requires the input from the educator (which may be you!). Maintaining a reflective eye and collaborating with other colleagues applies when using FL just as it would do when using other pedagogical approaches.

> "I make myself available to all students for individual, small group, and class feedback in real time as needed".

> "I conduct ongoing formative assessments during class time through observation and by recording data to inform future instruction".

> "I collaborate and reflect with other educators and take responsibility for transforming my practice".
> (Flipped Learning Network [FLN], 2014, p. 2)

Seeking to address all these aspects of the pillars at once and getting everything working smoothly from the offset is likely to be a challenging task. Breaking these parts down into the four sections and seeking to make small tweaks as you go along will enable you to ensure that the task is both manageable and staggered to allow for both you and your students to learn through the process of implementation.

Reflections on the benefits and challenges of adoption

The statements above could act as a starting point for considering some of your reflections of using FL. Additionally, through the adoption process, you might consider aspects that did not work so well, content that engaged your students more than others or adaptations that you would use in the future. This would not necessarily have to be a formal evaluation, but it could involve collating informal feedback from your students and reflections that you notice throughout your use.

Challenges and common obstacles

We know from the previous chapters that the benefits of using FL include student motivation, physical activity, and learning. Yet we are acutely aware that there are likely to be many challenges.

From the limited literature conducted in the context of PE, we know that challenges include insufficient avenues for students to develop their understanding and pre-class preparation being time consuming (Koh et al., 2020). In broader educational contexts, we know that educators have found other challenges such as creating a heavy workload for teachers and students, technical issues (Karabulut-Ilgu et al., 2018), students' familiarity with the approach, students' IT (Information Technology) resources at home and out of class support (Lo & Hew, 2017). Indeed, this is not an exhaustive list, and you may find many others along your adoption journey.

We think that one of the most common obstacles that you may face in your FL practice is students' view of the use of 'homework in PE'. We know from some of the literature conducted in this space that students might not expect PE homework or 'homework' in the traditional sense might only be used in examination PE (Hill, 2018; Smith & Madden, 2014). Furthermore, if your view in terms of the purpose of PE (as discussed in chapter 2) is for students to be physically active, then for students to be watching videos at home might seem counterintuitive to achieving this goal.

Another obstacle could be that the content and tasks that students complete independently at home are crucial to being able to cover certain content or learning when they return to class. As such, if a student does not complete their homework or is absent for a period then how will you ensure that they have the learning that they need to ensure they are not left behind? How will you know that the students have completed their home learning and gained the knowledge, understanding, or skills that you wanted them to? These may seem basic or trivial questions but considering them early on in your planning will mean that you are able to embed some of these aspects into your approach rather than seeking to address them at a later stage.

Support strategies

Considering all the elements covered above, the last part of this chapter looks at the different support strategies that can be implemented to help address or overcome some of these challenges. These will also be considered in the next chapter.

Using existing VLE structures, apps, or platforms that students are familiar with will help to ensure that students are focused on the task and not need to spend precious time on familiarising themselves with the different technologies and platforms. These structures may also have existing IT support to ensure that any problems that students have when they are away from school can be addressed. Similarly, having discussions to see if any IT support can be given to either you or the students may allow certain problems to be addressed to allow for the smooth running of your approaches.

Sargent and Casey (2020) discuss how seeking to establish consistency and routines of practice are a key enabler for FL. As such, thinking about elements that students use consistently and can become used to as just everyday routines of their experience of PE will help to support your practice. This may take time to develop and so this would not be a 'quick fix' solution. Indeed, it may even become part of your pedagogical approach. With the home environment being important for students to complete their learning tasks, working towards 'PE homework' becoming the norm for students may also form a part of establishing consistency and routines of practice. Communicating with your students' parents or guardians regarding the approach, what you are trying to achieve and what you expect of your students (and what they can expect from you in return!) may serve as a useful support strategy for your use of FL.

Having conversations with other colleagues at your school, different schools, or in areas such as social media can be a useful source of social support in terms of sharing different practices, techniques, reflections, or ideas. It may be that you are able to share tried and tested strategies and seek to gain knowledge regarding potential improvements that have worked in other contexts because of your conversation.

In this chapter, we have explored what happens when our ambitions for FL are implemented in practice. We have considered lots of reflective aspects for us to consider prior to, during, and after our implementation of FL. In the next chapter, we seek to take these aspects further in terms of providing some guiding principles for your practice as well as contextualising these within some case studies.

Questions for reflection

- What aspects do I need to consider pre, during, and after my use of flipped learning?
- How will I know that my use of flipped learning will be successful or not? What metrics am I using to judge its application in my classroom?
- What aspects of my teaching or students' learning am I seeking to address through my use of flipped learning? Do I need to adapt or focus on certain aspects of flipped learning to ensure that these aspects are being addressed?
- What technologies are appropriate in helping to support the application of this pedagogical approach?

References

Bergmann, J., & Sams, A. (2012). Before you flip, consider this. *Phi Delta Kappan, 94*(2), 25.

Birgili, B., Seggie, F. N., & Oğuz, E. (2021). The trends and outcomes of flipped learning research between 2012 and 2018: A descriptive content analysis. *Journal of Computers in Education, 8*(3), 365–394. doi:10.1007/s4 0692-021-00183-y

Brewer, R., & Movahedazarhouligh, S. (2018). Successful stories and conflicts: A literature review on the effectiveness of flipped learning in higher education. *Journal of Computer Assisted Learning, 34*(4), 409–416. doi:10.1111/jcal.12250

Dwivedi, Y. K., Rana, N. P., Jeyaraj, A., Clement, M., & Williams, M. D. (2019). Re-examining the Unified Theory of Acceptance and Use of Technology (UTAUT): Towards a revised theoretical model. *Information Systems Frontiers, 21*(3), 719–734. doi:10.1007/s10796-017-9774-y

Fairbairn, A. (2009). An integrated approach in designing and delivering courses using active learning pedagogies, engagement strategies, and technologies for the flipped classroom model. *Teaching and educational development institute, Sydney, Australia.* http://www.uq.edu.au/teach/flipped-classroom/docs/cs-fairbairn.pdf

Fletcher, T., Ní Chróinín, D., Gleddie, D., & Beni, S. (2021). *Meaningful physical education: An approach for teaching and learning.* Routledge.

Flipped Learning Network [FLN]. (2014). *Definition of flipped learning.* Retrieved from http://flippedlearning.org/domain/46

Hew, K. F., & Lo, C. K. (2018). Flipped classroom improves student learning in health professions education: A meta-analysis. *BMC Medical Education, 18*(1), 38. https://www.ncbi.nlm.nih.gov/pmc/articles/PMC5855972/pdf/12909_2018_Article_1144.pdf

Hill, K. (2018). Homework in physical education? A review of physical education homework literature. *Journal of Physical Education, Recreation & Dance, 89*, 58–63. doi:10.1080/07303084.2018.1440263

Karabulut-Ilgu, A., Jaramillo Cherrez, N., & Jahren, C. T. (2018). A systematic review of research on the flipped learning method in engineering education. *British Journal of Educational Technology, 49*(3), 398–411. doi:10.1111/bjet.12548

Koh, K. T., Li, C., & Mukherjee, S. (2020). Preservice physical education teachers' perceptions of a flipped basketball course: Benefits, challenges, and recommendations. *Journal of Teaching in Physical Education, 1*, 1–9. doi:10.1123/jtpe.2019-0195

Lo, C. K., & Hew, K. F. (2017). A critical review of flipped classroom challenges in K-12 education: Possible solutions and recommendations for future research. *Research and Practice in Technology Enhanced Learning, 12*(4), 1–22. doi:10.1186/s41039-016-0044-2

Lynch, S., & Sargent, J. (2020). Using the meaningful physical education features as a lens to view student experiences of democratic pedagogy in higher education. *Physical Education and Sport Pedagogy*, *25*(6), 629–642. doi:10.1080/17408989.2020.1779684

Østerlie, O. (2016). Flipped learning in physical education: Why and how? In D. Novak, B. Antala, & D. Knjaz (Eds.), *Physical education and new technologies* (pp. 166–176). Croatian Kinesiology Association. doi:10.13140/RG.2.2.19758.31048

Sargent, J., & Casey, A. (2020). Flipped learning, pedagogy and digital technology: Establishing consistent practice to optimise lesson time. *European Physical Education Review*, *26*, 70–84. doi:10.1177/1356336X19826603

Seery, M. K. (2015). Flipped learning in higher education chemistry: Emerging trends and potential directions. *Chemistry Education Research and Practice*, *16*(4), 758–768. doi:10.1039/c5rp00136f

Smith, M., & Madden, M. (2014). Middle school students' reactions to the implementation of active homework in physical education. *Global Journal of Health and Physical Education Pedagogy*, *3*(2), 121–136.

8   Guiding Principles for Flipped Learning in a Variety of Contexts

Flipped learning case studies

Case 1 – Middle school in the United States

The physical education (PE) context in the United States is largely dictated by broad state policies and local school districts' decisions on if and how to implement those policies (Killian et al., 2017). There are no national or state curriculum requirements, only suggested learning standards and grade-level outcomes, which carry weak or non-existent accountability oversight. As a result, teachers and their district colleagues largely dictate the content and learning opportunities students receive over the course of their primary and secondary PE experiences. The amount of time allocated for PE instruction varies widely and is generally limited to far less than the 150 minutes of weekly elementary school PE and 225 weekly minutes of secondary PE recommended by national organisations (Centers for Disease Control and Prevention [CDC], 2014). The generally hostile policy context in the United States inhibits the ability of PE teachers to positively influence students' achievement of program goals. Nevertheless, despite many challenges, the broad autonomy afforded PE teachers offers fertile ground for the adoption of innovative practices, like FL. Indeed, the PE context in the United States incentivises creative approaches to overcome the numerous barriers to adequate opportunities. The following case study illustrates the decision-making process of one middle school PE teacher who decided to apply FL to overcome less than ideal learning conditions in his school district.

Flipped learning (FL) was applied to an invasion games unit that integrated instructional strategies from the Teaching Games for Understanding model (TGU: Werner et al., 1996). The unit occurred as

DOI: 10.4324/9781003203377-10

part of a middle school boys' PE course in a high-poverty, high-density suburban school district in the Midwestern United States. The instructor in charge was Mr. Damon (pseudonym), who was in his 35th year of teaching and highly involved in professional development organisations. Due to the nature of the content and instruction for this set of lessons, Mr. Damon chose to use FL to introduce the key ideas for each lesson and provide demonstrations of activity formations and expectations before class. His primary motivation for use was to enhance the lessons by increasing the amount of time students had to participate in instructional games and learning-related small-group discussions. When he taught this content in previous years, he became frustrated with the amount of time he had to spend teaching and demonstrating skills, overviewing the activities, and managing student transitions into the activities. He understood that the bulk of learning in this unit occurred during students' active engagement in small-sided games and corresponding discussion. So, he sought to integrate FL as a solution to reduce large group instruction and management time, to give his students more time to engage in enhanced instructional gameplay and small group reflective conversations. This example represents Mr. Damon's initial iteration of FL (it is in line with what a Novice or Intermediate FL experience level teacher might develop. See Chapter 9 for more details). He deliberately designed the digital instruction using PowerPoint with embedded high-quality YouTube videos that demonstrated upcoming activities and posted all content on the school learning management system. These decisions were deliberate to minimise technology challenges and ensure the use of familiar programs and platforms for him and his students, in clear line with their technology comfort level.

Mr. Damon's school district had recently established a technology infusion initiative to encourage teachers to integrate learning-related digital tools into their courses. As part of the integration process, all students were provided with a free Google Chromebook, which they could use to engage with the digital content from their classes. Students were encouraged to complete any computer or Internet-based learning before, during study halls, or after school. Mr. Damon coordinated with homeroom teachers (sometimes called form tutors) to prompt his students to complete their flipped PE work during that time. Each day before the first class began, students at Mr. Damon's school had a 30-minute homeroom (sometimes called tutor) period where they were served breakfast, after which students had time to socialise or complete schoolwork. It was during this time that most of his students engaged with his FL PowerPoint information and assessments.

Welcome To The WSL
(Wentworth Soccer League)

Flipped Lesson for	Begins at:
Friday, April 28	Slide 2
Monday, May 1	Slide 7
Wednesday, May 3	Slide 12
Thursday, May 4	Slide 17
Friday, May 5	Slide 22
Monday, May 8	Slide 27

Figure 8.1 Main PowerPoint Slide with Links to Lesson Content.

For this flipped invasion games unit, Mr. Damon developed a PowerPoint that contained all the information for the unit split up into collections of slides, or modules, for each class. In this way, students could navigate the content of the unit according to their own preferences and needs, by looking ahead or returning to information as desired. Features of the PowerPoint program allowed students to click on a link for each specific class, which would take them directly to the relevant content for the next face-to-face class (Figure 8.1).

Modules were limited to key information students needed to know to successfully engage in practice and discussion opportunities during the subsequent class. These modules contained the knowledge and skills they would be practicing and applying during each lesson (Figure 8.2).

To accommodate students' different learning preferences, included in the slides were written explanations, as well as video demonstrations, of the instructional games students would be engaging in during the upcoming class. These activity slides also included key questions for students to think about while watching and primed students for the reflection points they would be discussing during teacher-facilitated small group breakout sessions (Figure 8.3).

The final slide of each module included a list of questions related to the information reviewed on the previous slides. These questions served as formative assessment opportunities for students to gauge their progress as well as an accountability measure to encourage students to engage with the content meaningfully. This measure was included to ensure they were prepared for class. Students were required

Invasion Game: *Skills*

Sending an Object: For example, throwing a ball or a disk, kicking a ball or passing a puck, ball or ring with the appropriate apparatus.

Receiving an object: For example, catching with the hands, cardling a ball with the feet, or receiving an object with a stick.

Dodging: Dodging typically refers to maintaining personal space, making sure not to collide with other players or objects.

Change of direction: Changing the direction your body is traveling is an extremely important skill to all games in this category.

Traveling in multiple directions: An important part on both the offensive and defensive side of these games is being mobile; going forwards, backwards, to either side, and to all diagonals.

Speed & Agility: An important skill in many games within the category of invasion/territory and in other categories as well.

Spatial awareness: Spatial awarness is a key concept within this category, and is usefull in many other categories. Through TFfU, students can easily develop the complicated skill of recognizing their position with association of the object of play (ball, Frisbee, etc) and their opponent. Spatial awarness might be one of the most important skills a student could possess when attempting to master more complex games.

Changes of speed: Being able to change speed is a skill as well as a strategy within the invasion category.

Anticipation: While anticipation is not a necessary skill it can be extremly valuable when playing defense in these types of games.

Footwork: Having good footwork will not improve balance, it will aid in learning all of the above skills.

(Griffin & Butler, 2005)

NEXT

Invasion Game: *Strategies*

How hard? (1 - 5)	Offensive strategy
1	Maintain Possession
2	Avoid defensive players
4	Create space for teammates
4	Create space for yourself
4	Attack goal

How hard? (1 - 5)	Defensive strategy
1	Defensive positioning
2	Playing area coverage
3	Gain Possession
4	Defend goal
5	Defend space
5	Predicting opponent's move

NEXT

Figure 8.2 Examples of Instructional Slides.

to complete the assessment and turn in their answers *prior to class* through their schools' learning management system, which allowed Mr. Damon to review the general level of his class' understanding. He could then tailor his face-to-face instruction based on student responses (Figure 8.4).

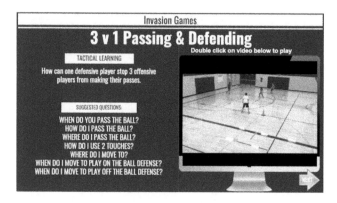

Figure 8.3 Examples of Instructional Slides with Written and Video Content.

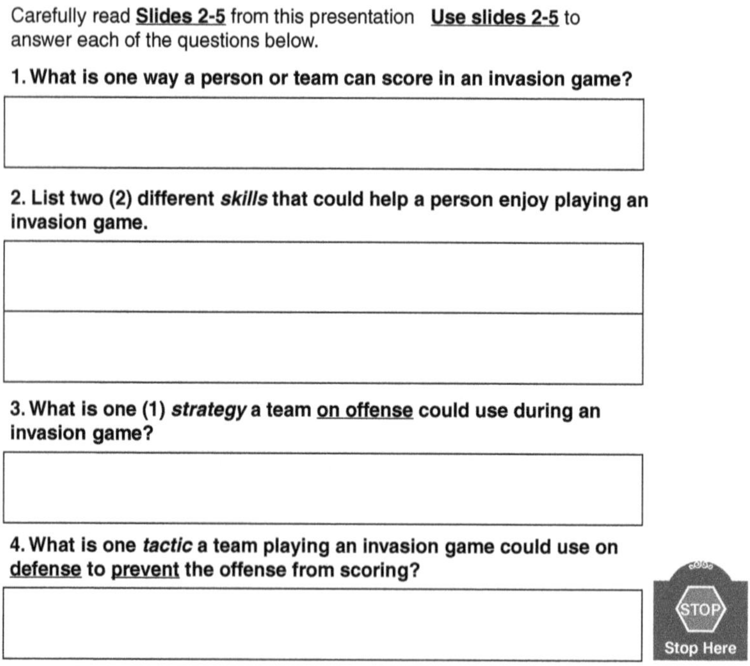

Carefully read **Slides 2-5** from this presentation   **Use slides 2-5** to answer each of the questions below.

1. What is one way a person or team can score in an invasion game?

2. List two (2) different *skills* that could help a person enjoy playing an invasion game.

3. What is one (1) *strategy* a team <u>on offense</u> could use during an invasion game?

4. What is one *tactic* a team playing an invasion game could use on <u>defense</u> to <u>prevent</u> the offense from scoring?

Figure 8.4 Examples of Assessment Slides.

During class, Mr. Damon was intentional about limiting his large group instruction. The activities he planned for each day corresponded directly to the information and videos he embedded within his PowerPoint modules. He would greet his students, offer any brief announcements, then prompt them into a practice or game play formation from the online module. Students would begin engaging in activity almost as soon as they entered the learning space from the locker room. As students were transitioning into their first activity, Mr. Damon would circulate through the learning space to offer targeted prompts intended to encourage students into the appropriate positions. He would also give any necessary corrective feedback to ensure the activity was performed as intended. During the practice activities and small-sided games, Mr. Damon would engage in small group discussions designed to prompt reflection on skills or strategies that might enhance their experience. These questions often came from the PowerPoint slides but were also extended to encourage thought specific to events occurring in the class. While he did this, all other groups continued practicing and playing, which contrasted previous classes where reflection was conducted as a large group where everyone played or discussed at the same time.

The culminating, summative assessment for the unit was delivered online. Students completed their test during homeroom, under the supervision of their homeroom teacher. This approach reduced all the challenges Mr. Damon previously experienced administering the paper/pencil test on a gym floor during class. Instead, students submitted their assessment through the learning management system where grading was expedited through digital tools and automated grading features. The effects of Mr. Damon's FL were an enhancement of in-class practice and small-sided gameplay opportunities for students.

Case 2 – Secondary school in Norway

The main aim of PE in Norway is to motivate all students to engage in a lifelong, physically active, and healthy lifestyle (The Norwegian Directorate for Education and Training, 2019). A recent report revealed that PE in Norwegian schools lacks variation both in content and teaching methods, and that this has resulted in a subject that is not beneficial for all students (Moen et al., 2018). Säfvenbom et al. (2014) reported a decline with age in student motivation to participate in PE, contrary to the intentions of the Norwegian PE curriculum. Motivation to participate in PE declines already from an early age and continues to decline throughout secondary school and upper secondary school. This decline is observed to be greater in adolescents than in young children and greater among girls than boys. The loss of motivation in Norwegian PE, especially among girls, is argued to partly be the result of a 'sportified' PE favouring boys and pupils who engage in sports outside school (Andrews & Johansen, 2005; Dowling, 2016; Säfvenbom et al., 2014). In Norway, a 'narrow' PE curriculum is observed regarding the subject content, where ball and fitness activities conducted in an instruction-conduction teaching manner seem to predominate (Moen et al., 2018). Moen et al. (2018) further state that PE students in Norway have expressed the wanting for more variations, and that they welcome alternative approaches to PE, laying the ground for successful implementation of an approach like FL.

In 2014, the idea of integrating theoretical/cognitive learning among PE students differently than in a traditionally theory class in a classroom spurred the idea of a research project looking into how digital technology could support student learning and motivation in PE (Østerlie, 2016, 2020). A researcher started then the making of a set of videos containing content regarding cognitive knowledge, connected to the national curriculum in Norwegian secondary PE. The result was three videos meant for use as preparation for three different classes. The topics were chosen based on the researcher and the research project teachers' perception of where lack of knowledge, and a desire for students to enter the practical learning situations with some more knowledge about the activities in a cognitive sense. This then resulted in an intervention connected to a research project at a teacher education facility in Mid-Norway during the winter of 2015. This intervention was based on constructivist approaches, emphasising that:

> Learning is an active process in which the individual seeks out information in relation to the task at hand and the environmental conditions prevailing at any given time and tests out her or his own capabilities within the context formed by the task and the environment. Learning is situated in social and cultural contexts and is influenced by these contexts.
>
> (Kirk & Macdonald, 1998, p. 376)

The intervention took place over a period of 3 weeks. Three learning resources about endurance, strength, and coordination were used. Each consisted of a video that was assigned for viewing as a homework task before class, an in-class lesson plan that the PE teacher followed, and a teacher's guide. The videos lasted about 12 minutes each and

Figure 8.5 Screenshot of the Video Elaborating on Strength Training.

were published on a digital learning platform which the students and teachers had access to. Each video gave a thorough but easy-to-understand introduction to the in-class topic. For example, when strength training was the weekly topic, the video explained muscular strength in a way appropriate to the age group by discussing why increased strength improves health, what happens in the body when the muscular strength is enhanced, and how to increase muscular strength (Figure 8.5).

At the end of the video, a summary of the forthcoming class content was given. Short quizzes embedded in the videos were used to increase the students' motivation to continue watching and to develop a deeper understanding of the content. The cooperation between the teacher involved in the research project and the researcher ensured that the in-class lesson was strongly linked to the video content and consisted of play-based activities focusing on one of the three topics in the intervention. The activities of the classes were also often based on cooperative work among students, in small groups, to promote discussion, reflection, and sharing of knowledge students had acquired prior to the class by watching the videos. This also aided students who had not prepared as fellow students in the group could explain and pass on information. In fact, several students found it fulfilling to take the role of 'teacher' and demonstrating or explaining aspects from the video content. The way this intervention was delivered, e.g., with the use of interaction details like a quiz in the video that also functioned as a guide to adjust face-to-face class content, would probably be characterised as an experienced level in terms of their use of FL (see Chapter 9 for further details).

Case 3 – Examination PE in the UK

In the UK, the subject of PE is delivered in a variety of different ways. For example, when students reach the latter part of their secondary education (ages 14–16, or what is termed grade or years 10 and 11), students can opt to take PE as a graded subject for their GCSE (General Certificate of Secondary Education) qualifications. After this time, they can select PE to study at A-Level in a college or 'sixth form' setting. Subsequently, at certain stages of students' educational experience, PE is structured in terms of an examination (often both written and practical) and obtaining a qualification based on a syllabus governed by the National Curriculum and the examination board. This is not the case in all school systems but is the context of this case study. The context of GCSE PE is the context of this case study using an AQA (formerly the Assessment and Qualification Alliance, it is an awarding body in the UK) exam specification. As such, FL was used to support the theoretical aspects of the written examination that students would undertake as part of their GCSE qualification and based upon some prior knowledge of students' understanding of the muscular and skeletal system.

This FL intervention was delivered by a teacher who had used some FL before but would probably be characterised as an intermediate level in terms of their use of FL (see Chapter 9 for further details) was utilised to support students' revision of key aspects of 'applied anatomy and physiology'. For this particular intervention, FL was applied to help support the specific aspects of the muscular and skeletal system. The teacher created a short video of 4 minutes long identifying the voluntary muscles involved in human movement (e.g., triceps, hamstrings). When discussing each muscle, the teacher provided a practical example of how they were being used in sport or physical activity (e.g., biceps – drawing a bow in archery). Students were then asked to contribute to an online Padlet wall adding the function of each muscle (e.g., biceps enable you to flex the elbow and bend the arm) and seeking to identify an alternative example of how they could be used in a sport/physical activity context. Students were able to comment and ask questions through the Padlet wall for the teacher to either respond to or add to a collaborative document that would be used at the start of the next lesson.

A similar function was used for the skeletal system whereby the main bones that make up the structure of the skeletal system identified through a short 2-minute video recorded by the teacher. A supplementary podcast was also used that students could refer to for an extension of the different descriptions of the bones. Students completed a short quiz of identifying the main functions of the skeletal system (i.e., movement, production of blood cells). The teacher then reviewed the students' answers to the quiz and reviewed the collective knowledge of the class. Aspects that students had struggled with in terms of their knowledge and understanding were incorporated at the start of the next class through group work whereby students worked in pairs to complete an interactive body of the muscular and skeletal system.

In reflecting upon their application of the use of FL in this case study, the teacher thought that the elements that worked well were students' collaboration in the online learning spaces and often providing peer support to each other. Areas for improvement were identified as needing to further support the routine of FL into the students' experience of PE.

A comparison of the three cases

What follows is a comparison of the cases in the sense of us trying to recognise what could be described as some of the common features of an FL approach across nations and (learning) cultures. This enables us to describe some guiding principles professionals should consider when planning to implement FL in their own practice. In Chapter 9, these principles will be elaborated on in terms of progression for you as a professional applying FL in PE.

Time. We recognise time to be a guiding principle in quality FL in PE. It is of great importance that the student (and their families) gets used to working in an FL fashion. As a more traditional approach to PE does not focus on learning but more on activity, as elaborated in Chapter 2, this is crucial for success. Time in terms of video length is also an issue to consider.

Preflection. In the preparational phase, the student must be presented with some content that enables the student to start thinking about what is to be learned in an upcoming PE class. This (un)intentional reflection started with watching, e.g., a video is called preflection (Jones & Bjelland, 2004; Wu et al., 2015) and is essential for a better learning outcome in the face-to-face PE class. The format of this preparational material is suggested to be a video, but also podcasts, PowerPoints, and text are possible formats.

Preparational format. The most used and preferred format of the material students should prepare is video. Length of the videos should be limited to uphold viewer attention, and interaction points throughout the video (e.g., quiz questions) are beneficial for attention, view time, and learning outcome. Nevertheless, to recognise high-quality FL in PE we suggest video format including interaction points.

Pre vs. in class. Students must feel that the time spent preparing prior to class is worthwhile. Hence, there must be a thorough connection between the material they use in the preparational phase and the experience in class content. This well-designed connection is crucial for the student's learning outcome and motivation in PE when implementing FL.

Policy. All learning activities need to derive from a national, regional, or local curriculum, so how you design your FL approach and content must be in line with these documents. This also includes considering regulations and policies on individual rights students have related to accessibility or universal design. In 2012, the Center for Inclusive Design and Environmental Access at the University at Buffalo expanded the definition of the principles of universal design to include social participation and health and wellness.

Teacher role in class. As time traditionally used for instructions is freed up, the teacher in an FL environment has time to be more attentive to students in their learning during the in-class time in PE. This prompts opportunities for feedback, assessment, and building relationships.

Guiding principles for achieving high-quality FL in PE

In Figure 8.6, we seek to characterise some of the guiding principles for achieving high-quality FL in PE. These are by no means an exhaustive list of aspects and you may well adapt and change this over time. Indeed, as you will see in the next chapter, the process of how to implement and consider some of these areas in terms of pre-, mid-, and post-flip phases are discussed as well as considering your own experiences of FL.

Quality Flipped Learning in Physical Education

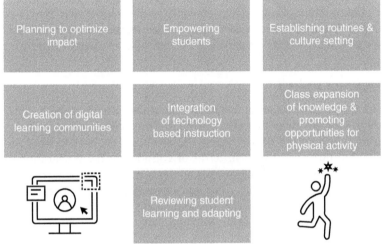

Figure 8.6 Guiding Principles of FL in PE.

Planning to optimise impact

This guiding principle relates to the teacher or educator planning to optimise impact – the impact in this sense could be students' understanding or application of a particular concept. Preflection in this sense comes into this phase as well as considering the preparational format and what policies will inform your planning. In FL, you want to make the most of the time that students are spending outside of the classroom. Therefore, structuring how students are going to spend their time at home, how much time they are spending on certain activities, and what you expect them to be able to do as a result of these activities will help guide your application of FL to make the most of the different learning spaces you are utilising.

Establishing routines and culture setting

An important principle for creating high-quality FL in PE is aiming towards establishing FL into the routines and culture of the classroom. This is particularly relevant to the idea of students' completed work or undertaking tasks outside the classroom space in terms of what might traditionally be called 'homework'. The preparational format of such homework could come into this phase in terms of the format and function of the home activities. Students may provide resistance at first to the idea of completing tasks at home yet if you can work towards the guiding principles of aiding students to understand why they are doing such activities and what it adds to their learning experience then you can build towards establishing FL into your classroom culture.

Empowering students

From the content we select, create, or ask students to work with, they should seek to give students ownership and independence in their learning. As with the above section, this also connects back to what we see within our case studies in terms of considering the preparational format of the content. Empowering students might also include other aspects which give students voice and ownership over their learning. For example, you might design the assessment with your students, or provide opportunities for leadership and personal responsibility.

Creation of digital learning communities and integration of technology-based instruction

This principle involves considering the pre vs. in-class phase in terms of sectioning out different activities and designing tasks appropriately. The teacher's role in class is of key importance in this principle. This is because of their support in terms of ensuring the students know what they are to be doing and when is crucial for the success of FL. For example, you may seek to integrate some technology-based instruction in class to help students familiarise with the platforms you are using or draw on existing platforms that students are using in other subjects or aspects of school.

Seeking to create digital learning communities by aiming to use technologies that you and your students are comfortable with, fit the purpose of the activity and one that they can interact with each other and the teacher. Drawing on the support and interaction of parents/ guardians, other classes or teachers can also help to build the members of the community.

Class expansion of knowledge, reviewing student learning and understanding

What is covered under this principle will be different depending on the length and structure of your activities. For example, reviewing students' learning and understanding is interwoven into your activities either through your assessment of their learning, their assessments, or what tasks/activities they can complete. We think a key principle is making sure that what is covered in class and home expands students' knowledge. Students will need to see the progression, value, and motivation for completing the different activities and different spaces.

We believe that these principles act as an underpinning focus to ensure the high-quality use of FL in PE. We seek not to distinguish what is or is not FL but provide fluid principles for you to work within and towards.

In the next chapter, we seek to take these principles a step further in considering various levels of experience with FL and consider the different phases of how to get started with the learning process.

Questions for reflection

- What aspects of the case studies resonate with my own experience? Where do they differ and why?
- What aspects of the guiding features of flipped learning do I think are the most important for me to consider?
- Which aspects come in the case studies do I currently meet and which one(s) could I work towards addressing in my practice?

References

Andrews, T., & Johansen, V. (2005). Gym er det faget jeg hater mest. *Norsk Pedagogisk Tidsskrift*, *89*(04), 302–314.

Centers for Disease Control and Prevention [CDC]. (2014). *State indicator report on physical activity, 2014*. Department of Health and Human Services. http://www.cdc.gov/physicalactivity/downloads/pa_state_indicator_report_2014.pdf

Dowling, F. (2016). De idrettsflinkes arena: Ungdoms fortellinger fra kroppsøvingsfaget med blikk på sosial klasse. In Ø. Seippel, M. K. Sisjord, & Å. Strandbu (Eds.), *Ungdom og Idrett* (pp. 249–268). Cappelen Damm akademisk.

Jones, L. B., & Bjelland, D. (2004). International experiential learning in agriculture. Proceedings of the 20th Annual Conference, Association for International Agricultural and Extension Education (AIAEE), Dublin, Ireland.

Killian, C. M., Graber, K. C., & Woods, A. M. (2017). Elementary physical education in the United States: Policies and practice. In D. Colella, B. Antala, & S. Epifani (Eds.), *Physical education in primary school: Researches-best practices-situation* (pp. 403–413). Pensa Multimedia Editore.

Kirk, D., & Macdonald, D. (1998). Situated learning in physical education. *Journal of Teaching in Physical Education*, *17*(3), 376–387.

Moen, K. M., Westlie, K., Bjørke, L., & Brattli, V. H. (2018). *Når ambisjon møter tradisjon: En nasjonal kartleggingsstudie av kroppsøvingsfaget i grunnskolen (5.–10. trinn)* (Oppdragsrapport nr. 1–2018). Høgskolen i Innlandet. https://brage.bibsys.no/xmlui/handle/11250/2482450

Østerlie, O. (2016). Flipped learning in physical education: Why and how? In D. Novak, B. Antala, & D. Knjaz (Eds.), *Physical education and new technologies* (pp. 166–176). Croatian Kinesiology Association. doi:10.13140/RG.2.2.19758.31048

Østerlie, O. (2020). *Flipped learning in physical education: A gateway to motivation and (deep) learning* [Doctoral thesis, Norwegian University of Science and Technology]. Trondheim. https://hdl.handle.net/11250/2649972

Säfvenbom, R., Haugen, T., & Bulie, M. (2014). Attitudes toward and motivation for PE: Who collects the benefits of the subject? *Physical Education and Sport Pedagogy*, *20*(6), 629–646. doi:10.1080/17408989.2014.892063

The Norwegian Directorate for Education and Training. (2019). *Curriculum in physical education (KRO01-05)*. https://www.udir.no/lk20/kro01–05

Werner, P., Thorpe, R., & Bunker, D. (1996). Teaching games for understanding: Evolution of a model. *Journal of Physical Education, Recreation & Dance*, *67*(1), 28–33. doi:10.1080/07303084.1996.10607176

Wu, L., Ye, X., & Looi, C.-K. (2015). Teachers' preflection in early stages of diffusion of an innovation. *Journal of Computers in Education*, *2*(1), 1–24. doi:10.1007/s40692-014-0022-x

9 How Do I Start with Flipped Learning in Physical Education, and Where Could It Lead?

Flipped learning (FL) in many ways departs from the standard methods by which physical education (PE) is done. It adds layers of effort for teachers and students beyond direct instruction and multi-activity PE. As a result, thinking about flipping a PE curriculum or even an entire unit of content might seem intimidating, impossible, or irrelevant to PE teachers, given the many daily tasks and challenges they face. During FL, direct instruction is replaced to give space for students to learn content more deeply through overlapping digital and applied learning opportunities. Students develop their knowledge, skills, and attitudes through combinations of student-centred, digital and in-person learning opportunities. The use of digital technology to facilitate learning requires supporting school policies to ensure equity when it comes to students' access to learning devices, strong Wi-Fi, and time to engage with digital content. Transitioning towards a more robust FL learning culture requires extra support for students and positive socialisation experiences that motivate them to engage meaningfully in FL opportunities, especially if they are not accustomed to deep, asynchronous learning opportunities in PE. More in-depth teaching and learning processes within FL may increase the planning and implementation burden on teachers, particularly as a result of the infusion of digital technology. Despite the differences and challenges associated with FL (and the integration of any new pedagogical approach), we hope that previous chapters have demonstrated how FL can be a valuable addition to PE curricula. In light of this, we suggest taking a step-by-step approach when beginning to infuse FL. Iterating from basic to more in-depth uses of FL is likely a much more appropriate and feasible way to start adding FL experiences into PE programs for most.

This chapter details information PE teachers can use to reflect on whether they should even use FL, where it might be most applicable within their curriculums, and how to begin using FL in a manageable way. We suggest a step-by-step process beginning with a focus on the pre-flip

DOI: 10.4324/9781003203377-11

formatting aspects of FL, particularly for teachers who are novice to the FL approach. We then share intermediate ways teachers might progress to using pre- and mid-flip teaching actions and then advance towards experienced pre-, mid-, and post-flip strategies. We end this chapter with an overview of what a fully integrated FL program might look like.

Throughout the chapter, we suggest appropriate policies, ways to evolve towards a PE learning culture, and teaching processes essential to support robust and rigorous FL in PE at various stages of teacher comfort and experience. But, we recognise advocating for policy change takes time if the suggested policies are not currently in place at your school. Developing learning culture takes patience, especially if students are used to just playing games. Fine-tuning teaching processes to align with FL takes effort and reflection. So, we suggest teachers start small, iterate, and develop FL step-by-step over time. Identify aspects of FL that can be adopted more easily and work from there. Apply a reflective, action research-oriented approach to see what happens before, during, and after one flipped lesson. Then, build on the positives and rework the negatives (Figure 9.1).

The staircase graphic illustrates one example of how a teacher might *begin* to think about FL and *start the process* of iterating towards comprehensive integration of FL into a unit of instruction or their entire program. The graphic depicts a staircase to emphasise the progressive approach of adopting FL across each of the components of FL. The different steps offer action points for teachers to consider and reflect on during each phase of integration. These may be considered sequentially or individually, as aspects of multiple steps might be applicable to your context right away. The key is taking a thoughtful approach to applying FL appropriately according to your own contexts.

Considerations for novices or how to begin iterating: Focus on the pre-flip

The first step represents the pre-flip phase or what happens before face-to-face active application of learning gleaned through digital instruction. For a teacher who is new to FL, focusing on the pre-flip aspects of the FL process will likely be a manageable place to start, as it tends to attend more to the planning side of the process.

Determine student readiness and support for digital learning in PE

The first step of planning is determining whether students are even ready to use FL then acting accordingly. For example, teachers of young

PRE-FLIP	PRE-MID-FLIP	PRE-MID-POST-FLIP	PRE-MID-POST-FLIP, plus POLICIES & LEARNING CULTURE
• Determine student readiness and household support for digital learning • Identify a lesson that contains a lot of direct instruction • Use existing digital resources to find a high-quality video that demonstrates the skill or overviews the concept emphasized in the lesson • Support students' buy-in and use of FL • Assign students to watch the video and complete a short, simple assignment prior to class • Apply an action research approach by reflecting and identifying what works and what can/should be improved during further iterations	• Identify a series of lessons that are more complex or contain a lot of direct instruction • Use existing digital resources to find high quality videos or podcasts that demonstrate the skill(s), concepts, and/or strategies emphasized in the lessons • Consider developing one or more of the videos/podcasts on your own or with your teaching team • Assign students to watch the videos and/or listen to the podcasts prior to each class • Develop social/collaborative assessments to encourage quality reflection and interaction related to digital content • Apply an action research approach by reflecting and identifying what works and what can/should be improved during further iterations	• Identify a unit or units of study that might benefit from FL • Use existing digital resources to find high quality videos or podcasts that demonstrate the skill(s), concepts, and/or strategies emphasized in the lessons • Design high quality digital resources for use across the unit(s) • Assign students to watch the videos and/or listen to the podcasts prior to each class • Develop social/collaborative assessments to encourage quality reflection and interaction related to the digital content • Create face-to-face applied active learning opportunities for students to apply digital content • Establish routines that quickly and actively engage students in applied learning • Review assessments prior to classes and adjust content according to student understanding, as possible • Apply an action research approach by reflecting and identifying what works and what can/should be improved during further iterations	• Advocate and enact policies that support equitable student learning with and through digital technology • Establish a culture and environment of deep learning • Identify a unit or units of study that might benefit from FL • Use existing digital resources to find high quality videos or podcasts that demonstrate the skill(s), concepts, and/or strategies emphasized in the lessons • Design high quality digital resources for use across the unit(s) • Promote at-home physical activity engagement and encourage students to invite household members • Assign students to watch the videos and/or listen to the podcasts prior to each class • Develop social/collaborative assessments to encourage quality reflection and interaction related to the digital content • Create face-to-face applied active learning opportunities for students to apply digital content • Establish routines that quickly and actively engage students in applied learning • Review assessments prior to classes and adjust content according to student understanding, as possible • Apply an action research approach by reflecting and identifying what works and what can/should be improved during further iterations
Novice	Intermediate	Experienced	Ideal

Figure 9.1 The FL in PE Level Staircase.

students may not feel their students are developmentally prepared to autonomously engage in digital learning or lack enough household support to help them engage. Similarly, teachers in schools where the homework and/or digital learning burden is already extreme may not want to contribute to student stress levels with outside work at this time. In situations such as these, we recommend working to advocate and support for positive changes, so the context becomes more favourable to using FL in PE. For example, you might identify ways to inform and engage households to support FL in PE or promote collective decision-making with other subject area teachers to balance the homework burden.

Questions to consider in determining student readiness and support are as follows:

- To what extent have my students engaged with FL in other subjects?
- To what extent does my school support digital learning?
- What is the general level of household involvement in supporting student (digital) learning?

For teachers who have determined their students are ready and capable of engaging autonomously with digital instruction in FL or have adequate household support to help them do so, they can then begin to think about planning the best way to integrate and iterate FL into their local programs.

Choose lessons that will maximise FL benefits

Planning for PE lessons is always essential to maximise learning opportunities for students regardless of whether FL is applied or not. Students are meant to be active during PE and a key benefit of applying FL is the corresponding increase in active-learning time it affords in class. So, as you begin to think about which lesson or lessons to flip first and where FL might provide value to your program, perhaps begin by considering the following questions:

- What existing content contains a lot of direct instruction?
- Which lessons are students listening more than they are active?
- Is there information students consistently need repeating?

Since digital instruction takes the place of direct instruction with FL, asking these types of questions can help identify areas where FL could provide the most benefit and offer a sensible starting point to help identify possible lesson(s) to flip.

Identify existing, high-quality digital resources for content delivery

Once you have identified a lesson or lessons that is/are heavy on direct instruction (and less student activity, as a result), the next thing to begin thinking about is how to best transfer direct instruction online. The internet can be a helpful place to find quality digital content, especially for teachers intimidated by the thought of making/editing/sharing their own digital content or those burdened by heavy teaching and extra-curricular and life responsibilities. A good place to start is finding existing digital resources that cover the essential material. So, consider asking:

- What digital content (e.g., videos, podcasts, articles) already exists that could be used to adequately prepare students for in-class activities?
- Is the content thorough, aligned with my curriculum, and delivered in a manner relatable to and developmentally appropriate for my students?

There is a wide range of digital resources available that provide free and appropriate instruction across content areas (Goad et al., 2019; Lanier et al., 2021). Providing essential content through 'brokering' or 'curating' allows for more efficient development of FL, especially in the early stages of integration, and eliminates the burden of independently developing high-quality digital instruction. Nevertheless, it will require you to rigorously preview the material and become familiar with it to ensure it provides adequate instruction and preparation for your students, especially if using social media instruction from websites like YouTube, TikTok, or Facebook.

Supporting students' buy-in and use of FL in PE

One key support mechanism for students' online learning is 'ease of use' and familiarity with the learning management system (LMS) or platform (Killian & Woods, 2021), so, consider asking:

- What LMS does my school use?
- What are common learning applications students might be familiar with?

Use technologies familiar to students and ones that are aligned with broader school approaches. If possible, try to avoid using novel learning Apps, platforms, and programs unless there is appropriate introduction and support prior to their use. For example, using Google Classroom as your platform for digital instruction while your school uses Canvas or Blackboard may cause unnecessary challenges for students. Using platforms and technologies familiar to students will limit barriers to teaching and learning (at least initially), especially for students new to FL in PE. As a result, it is likely that you and your students will spend less time learning about the functions of the technology and more focus can be spent on the content.

The next consideration is determining how to support student transition to using FL in PE and promote buy-in to the processes and value of FL. To maximise the positive benefits of FL, teachers need to ensure there is student 'buy-in'. In other words, students generally need to understand the value of FL and the reasons behind its use, to want to engage with the digital aspects prior to class (Killian & Woods, 2021). It is up to teachers to determine the best ways to help them realise it, otherwise FL just becomes another homework task rather than a valuable tool to support meaningful engagement and learning. How you help your students understand the value of FL will differ depending on their relationship with students, students' readiness to use technology to support their learning, and the digital venues teachers choose.

Embedding simple assignments and assessments

When beginning the use of FL from a novice perspective and focusing on the pre-flip aspect of the FL process, consider using the first few digital instruction assignments as a way to help socialise students into the FL process. These initial independent digital learning experiences can serve as practice or priming opportunities for students (and teachers) that can act to demonstrate expectations for more in-depth FL students might engage in during future iterations. Consider thinking about:

• How much time do students need to complete PE FL assignments?
• What kind of opportunities can I provide to demonstrate expectations and support students' appropriate engagement with digital assignments?

So, give students ample time to engage with the digital content and consider building in brief reflection assignments or short multiple-choice quizzes based on the video content. You might even consider allotting class time for students to navigate the first or several digital assignments, so they can collaborate or peer coach each other and so you are available to provide feedback and assist with learning system navigation. Also consider seeking students' input regarding their perceptions and experiences of engaging with FL as you designed it. This can be done by building in a brief survey or open-ended questions at the end of a brief content quiz or assignment. The information you obtain through their feedback could then inform your reflective process and offer key feedback for future design considerations and iterations.

Apply an action research approach

Ultimately the first few iterations of FL will be a novel experience for both you and your students. For many, taking it slow is the best approach. Focus on the pre-flip, planning components and use each part of the process we just discussed as a learning experience. Approach it from an action research perspective and at each stage seek to determine (both from your own observations, as well as students' perspectives):

- What is working well (from your own and students' lenses)?
- What can I improve to make this a more enriching experience for my students (and me)?

Keep doing the things that work. Adjust the things that do not. And when you are ready, you can begin to think about adding a layer to your FL approach by starting to think about and integrating mid-flip aspects of the process.

Considerations for intermediate users or how to continue iterating: Building on the pre-flip

The Mid-Flip phase is the next step for teachers who are ready to progress after focusing on developing foundational pre-flip aspects of the process for a bit. It is also a good step to begin for teachers with an intermediate level of experience with FL who might have a firm foundation of pre-flip components in place already. The mid-flip step is what happens after digital content is assigned and before face-to-face application of learning occurs in class. It still emphasises the integration of the FL format, but represents an elevated iteration from the novice step, so you can begin to build on your work establishing pre-flip rhythms. You can start to connect previous individual digital lessons to create a series of FL lessons or even construct a complete unit. Remember, try to identify a series of lessons that contain more

complex instruction or a series of lessons that have a lot of direct instruction to maximise the benefits of FL to students.

Practice developing your own digital content

At this step, you might start to think about trying to cultivate your
own technology skills. This might include beginning to develop your
digital instruction library by creating some basic digital content for a
lesson or two of the series or unit you have chosen to flip. Of course,
using existing digital content from is still likely more efficient, there is
value to recording your own voice or using images of yourself to demonstrate skills, at least for a portion of the content. Students know
you and, in many ways, can relate better to a familiar, trustworthy
digital teaching presence. So, consider the following questions, as you
decide if and how you might approach learning new technology skills
or building your current digital content library:

*   What technology skills do I currently possess?
*   What programs am I most familiar with?
*   How comfortable am I learning new skills?
*   What level of support does my school provide for teachers seeking
    to learn technology skills?
*   Do I have a social network of teachers who might collaborate with
    me to develop digital content together?

Answers to these questions will determine how you go about developing your skills and digital content. Familiar applications like
Microsoft PowerPoint allow voice recording over slides. There are
many freely available video recording and editing programs like
Screencast-O-Matic (https://screencast-o-matic.com), that offer easy-
to-use content development platforms. These programs often provide
in-depth 'how to' tutorials. There is also a wide range of tutorial videos
on social media platforms, like Twitter and YouTube, that offer step-
by-step guides to making engaging content with commonly available
programs and applications. Digital content development does not have
to be an individual pursuit. Consider learning and partnering with a
colleague or colleagues to create a video or podcast series of digital
content for a unit or link up with Information Technology support
staff at your school for support during construction. These initial videos can be simple (see Case #1 from Chapter 8) and are really about
helping you gain confidence for more in-depth content development
down the road.

Developing and embedding richer assignments and assessments

Assessment is key to the teaching and learning process in PE. It also provides a layer of accountability within FL. Using assessments to evaluate student understanding of digital content allows you to formatively assess knowledge and gauge student engagement with the asynchronous portion of FL. The assessment also provides a layer of accountability for students to motivate them to actually prepare for in-class application of the content when FL is fully implemented. Simple quizzes can fulfil this role and represent a good starting place for Intermediate Users, particularly because many LMSs have automated grading features, which help with time management. However, implementing reflective and/or social assessments may offer students a more valuable, engaging learning experience as your students and you become more accustomed to the FL approach. So, this step might be a good time to begin building on the simple assessments assigned during the pre-flip/novice step to include more rich and reflective assessments *for* learning (for ideas, see Feith (2017)).

Considerations for experienced teachers or how to more fully implement FL

Teachers experienced with FL are ones who have iteratively built on the pre- and mid-flip phases of the FL process and are ready to apply FL more broadly within a unit or units of instruction. This is also the step where you can begin to connect in-class applied learning opportunities with the digital content you have been assigning, which means this is the step where your FL process transitions to a student-centred approach, rather than just an integration of the FL instructional format. Up until this point, the process has focused on embedded the FL format into your instruction to help you and your students get used to digital learning as a component of PE. So, at this 'Experienced' step, your students should be ready for independent learning and well-adjusted to the expectations and processes of asynchronous digital learning engagement within FL. You should be getting comfortable identifying high-quality existing digital content as well as developing your own. The next thing to begin thinking about now is how you might start to connect in-class learning opportunities to the digital instruction in ways that encourage social application of the content. This aspect of the process adds an additional layer of planning for you to consider.

- How can you plan in-class active learning opportunities that encourage effective application of students' digital learning without just repeating or reteaching what students are supposed to have already learned through their asynchronous learning?

After all, if you repeat the instruction or demonstrations contained in the digital content during live classes, then FL just becomes a homework burden for students (and teachers) with limited positive impact on live active learning. Intentional planning for FL in PE is therefore essential to maximise the benefits of the approach.

Plan with a (the FL) purpose in mind

Similar to previous steps, planning with a purpose is helpful to maximise the impact of FL. Start by choosing or building on content heavy in direct instruction, so students absorb the motivational, learning, PA, social benefits of FL. You can begin this process by asking yourself:

* What do students need to know to be able to appropriately participate in the connected in-class active learning opportunities?
* What does the digital instruction need to include so students are prepared for face-to-face applied learning activities?

Content to include in digital instruction might be skill cues and performance demonstrations, rule overviews of a new small-sided game or group activity, strategic insights for upcoming games, illustrations of the learning formations students will encounter during class, and/or essential questions for reflection. It is ultimately up to you, the teacher or educator, to determine what content will best prepare students for your planned face-to-face learning. But, by thinking about where most of your planned talking comes from during class (i.e., demonstrating skills and strategy, and explaining rules and formations), you can identify aspects of lessons you might be able to transition online. From there, you can start to synthesise in-class lessons with the digital content you curated or developed by determining how to connect prework to in-class opportunities, for optimal impact. Ask:

* What did students learn through the digital instruction I have developed or curated?
* What activities will support appropriate skill and knowledge application in alignment with the corresponding digital content?

These questions will help you develop in-class learning opportunities that emphasise students' pre-work digital learning and formative assessment. From there, it is time to decide what the learning processes will look like in class to ensure and maximise appropriate application of the digital content.

Establish routines for optimal impact

Optimal impact means using FL to maximise active learning. This begins with deciding how to best begin and operate an FL class to provide maximum opportunities for students to actively engage. Depending on the content, there may be value in offering concrete review of some essential digital content, so you might start by asking yourself:

• What aspects of the digital content would students benefit from reviewing during live class?
• Might there be ways you can prompt students immediately into small group or individual activities and provide feedback from there?

The answers to these questions depend on the nature and comprehensiveness of the digital instruction and the routines you choose to enact during face-to-face classes. If you find yourself needing to repeat a lot of the content from the digital instruction, you may want to rethink how you develop that aspect of your FL material to better prepare students. If possible, also try to review student engagement with the digital content and assessments as well to understand whether they are appropriately interacting with important information prior to arriving in class. In any case, a key for teachers during this step is to only repeat essential information and try to avoid repeating the bulk of instruction that students should have already engaged with during their pre-work digital learning. Otherwise, the digital component becomes less valuable and likely just a homework burden for students, particularly if they know all the digital content will just be repeated during class anyway. So, find ways to quickly encourage students into active learning at the beginning of class. From there, you can evaluate students' understanding and performance through observation, feedback, peer teaching, and small group discussions.

Tailor active learning based on student assignment/assessment performance

A valuable component of FL is the capacity for teachers (and students) to conduct asynchronous, formative assessments prior to face-to-face classes. This allows you, the teacher, to review student understanding and possibly tailor your instruction to accommodate student mastery in real time. The most basic way to use these FL formative assessment data is to decide what content students might benefit from reviewing during class and in how much detail. Consider asking:

- What is the extent of student understanding of digital content as demonstrated by their performance on formative digital assessments and/or assignments?
- Based on formative assessment/assignment performance, what content (if any) should be reviewed in class?
- What in-class activities can I adjust to make sure learning activities align with their mastery?

If most students achieve a satisfactory score on a quiz you assigned, you might be able to prompt them into an activity with less review than if a lot of students performed poorly, in which case you would likely want to take more time to repeat the content before they engage in the activity. For example, at the beginning of a manipulative skills unit, you might introduce students to basic grip of a short-handed implement during your video content then plan several individual striking activities at the onset of the next class. Your assessment might include students taking a picture of themselves using the appropriate grips and cues, then posting it to the LMS discussion board for you and/or peers to offer encouragement and feedback. If students in one class show a similar grip error in their photos, you might begin the class with an active review of the grips before transitioning into the striking activities you originally had planned. If students in another class show generally appropriate grips in their photos, you might begin the class with the striking activities as originally planned. Using the FL formative assessment data can help you adjust your instruction according to student understanding.

A holistic, comprehensive FL approach

The highest step of the FL iteration represents an ideal scenario for deep, integrated FL in PE. Teachers operating at this step have extensive experience with FL and/or have progressed through the iteration process from the novice/pre-flip step, to the pre-mid flip Intermediate step, to the pre-mid-post flip experienced step all the way up to an 'Ideal step'. The Ideal step includes some contextual aspects and strategies that do not necessarily have to be in place for FL to occur, but nevertheless provide solid, added support layers for student learning in and beyond the gym. The policies and considerations we suggest here may be advocated and enacted at any step of your process and hopefully your school already offers broader support for digital learning beyond the gymnasium.

Digital learning policies

In educational contexts where digital learning is enacted, digital learning policies are important safeguards that should facilitate students' free access to equitable engagement with technology-based instruction. In other words, if schools and/or teachers embed digital instruction like FL within their curriculums, certain policy supports should be in place to ensure equitable learning opportunities for all students. The degree to which technology is infused into PE curriculums globally varies, therefore the strength of digital learning policies in schools are likely broad, as well. FL can occur in any school regardless of the technology policies in place. Yet, in an ideal world, the following policy suggestions would be in place prior to implementing FL in PE. However, if these policies do not yet exist in your school, they represent key aspects for which you can iterate and advocate towards. Several key policy questions to consider are as follows:

- Does my school provide students with digital learning devices (i.e., iPads, laptops) or offer access to such devices (i.e., in a library or a digital learning lab)?
- Does my school provide students with access to quality Wi-Fi?
- Is there supervised time before, during, and/or after school for students to engage in digital learning assignments?
- Does my school require teacher and student adherence to data security protocols?

If the answer to any of these questions is no, the potential for inequitable digital learning opportunities exists for students who may not have access to digital learning devices at home, or for students without reliable Wi-Fi connections where they live. It is therefore important for schools to offer devices and time for students to engage in digital learning to ensure all students are supported and have access to equitable, ideal (flipped) learning opportunities.

Leverage digital instruction to promote at-home physical activity and household engagement

Experienced (and perhaps Novice and Intermediate) FL teachers are likely ready to think intentionally about how they might leverage digital instruction to promote at-home physical activity and skill practice, as well as invite and engage household members into PE learning. Due to its asynchronous nature, digital instruction can help breakdown school time boundaries and allow you to support whole school initiatives to promote physical activity opportunities beyond the school day (Chapter 4). The type of content you choose to deliver digitally will dictate the appropriateness of promoting at-home physical activity and skill practice and whether family or household members can/should be invited into at-home learning activities by students. For example, if the content you preview on video requires a lot of highly specialised equipment (i.e., weight training safety, rock wall climbing etiquette), it probably is not going to be appropriate or even possible to promote at-home physical activity engagement. But just because all students might not have access to the exact equipment they use during class, you can still encourage at-home practice. A wide variety of resources for at-home PE were developed during the COVID-19 pandemic and many include equipment substitutes, which can help you identify common household items students can use to practice skills and play games (Gopher Community, 2020).

Many of you may choose to find and use quality digital content that already exists, which is efficient and appropriate for FL, but also static. The content you find online may not be designed specifically for PE or at-home and, therefore, might not offer alternative equipment ideas or intentionally prompt students to invite family or household members into practice opportunities. If this is the case, you might consider adding a slide or including a supplemental document describing ways students can use household equipment and encouraging them to try practicing with someone at home. However, you choose to encourage at-home PE engagement, be sure to consider using various ways to encourage family and household involvement. For example, you could encourage students to practice by tossing and catching an object with another person. Another time, you might encourage students to teach a skill to a family member or recite skill cues for performing skill to someone else. The wonderful thing about FL is it gives you opportunities to encourage students to participate in instructional physical activity beyond the gym. Offer them fun and creative ways they can be active at-home and be intentional about encouraging them to invite others to participate with them (if and when appropriate)!

This chapter provides a sequence of iterations towards an ideal integration of FL into PE for you to consider. However, we recognise that FL will look different depending on a wide range of factors. Our intention is not for our steps to offer a prescription or recipe that, if followed, will result in perfect FL implementation. Rather, we hope our suggestions will be taken into account through your own teaching lenses. Ultimately, you know yourself, your students, your schools, and your communities best. Use a reflective, iterative approach and happy flipping!

References

Feith, J. (2017, Dec 07). The #PhysEd Show Podcast [Audio podcast episode]. *Assessment for learning in physical education.* https://thephysicaleducator. com/2017/12/07/assessment-for-learning/

Goad, T., Towner, B., Jones, E., & Bulger, S. (2019). Instructional tools for online physical education: Using mobile technologies to enhance learning. *Journal of Physical Education, Recreation & Dance, 90*(6), 40–47. doi:10. 1080/07303084.2019.1614118

Gopher Community. (2020). At-home equipment replacement list. *PE Blog.* https://blog.gophersport.com/at-home-equipment-replacement-list/

Killian, C. M., & Woods, A. M. (2021). Physical education students' usage and perceptions of a supplemental online health-related fitness knowledge curriculum (iPE). *European Physical Education Review,* 1–18. doi:10. 1177/1356336X211065953

Lanier, K. V., Killian, C. M., & Burnett, R. (2021). Integrating strength and conditioning into a high school physical education curriculum: A case example. *Journal of Physical Education, Recreation & Dance, 92*(5), 18–26. doi:10.1080/07303084.2021.1896401

10 Towards a Definition of Flipped Learning in Physical Education: Summary and Concluding Thoughts

In concluding this book, we summarise our key contributions to knowledge and the takeaway messages that we feel provide a significant ending to our writing. While this might be the last chapter of this book, we see this as the springboard for considering our practical use of flipped learning (FL) in physical education (PE).

Start small, aiming for high quality

In exploring the use of this approach within PE, the mantra of 'starting small' seems appropriate. By this, we mean making small tweaks and changes to your practice in seeking to trial FL. Changing too much (too quickly) is likely to cause overload but also a deviation from learning for both you and your students. As we have shown, small starting points might be one video that you seek to record. If it is of high quality (in terms of content rather than resolution!) and well planned then it is likely to get across the points you want to students, engage them in the learning, and allow you to meet your learning outcomes.

Seek to extend rather than replicate

Our focus in this book has been seeking to extend what we already know. This is similarly the case in considering your use of FL. Seeking to extend your own and students' knowledge outside of the space of the classroom (rather than replicate what you already do) will allow you to tap into some of the benefits for your students. Of course, it may be appropriate to sometimes replicate what you have done in the classroom to consolidate learning or to support the learning of different students. That being said, the general consideration is extending

DOI: 10.4324/9781003203377-12

students' learning time outside of the classroom rather than seeking to replicate their in-class experiences.

Champion the culture change and meaningful routine of 'homework'

Homework might have negative connotations for students. Changing how they view and the purpose of their home tasks in PE we believe is important for FL success. It can take time to embed the routine of 'homework' into students' experiences of PE. Classic examples from other subject areas such as ensuring students know the purpose of their homework, providing clear instructions/support, setting your expectations of students and their expectations of you are just some of the ways in which you can be a champion of normalising the use of home-based tasks in PE.

A working definition

In Chapter 3, we discussed the definitions and interpretations of FL. As we noted, these definitions have largely been constructed in STEM (Science Technology Engineering and Maths) subjects rather than subject areas such as PE. Based upon the emergent thoughts within this book, we use this space to provide a working definition that others can use as a basis for their thinking. We do not see this as an end point but rather the starting point for how we think about FL within the context of PE.

FL is a student-centred approach to learning which permeates before and during face-to-face classes which is supported by the format of using asynchronous (digital) instruction, closely related to the upcoming learning situations, to prime or inform student understanding of movement. Students are guided through learning material before and after class with the teacher-student contact time being used to deepen understanding of PE through discussion, problem-solving, and collaboration. With this in mind, we define:

> Flipped learning in physical education uses asynchronous digital instruction for the expansion of learning and the promotion of physical activity opportunities beyond the PE class and is designed to enrich students' skills and knowledge for upcoming face-to-face classes where they engage in collaborative, guided movement experiences designed to extend and deepen their prior learning.

In the sections below, each of the authors share some concluding reflections.

Ove

When I considered proposing to Routledge writing a book on FL in PE, I had just defended my dr.philos. thesis and was looking for a way to bring this topic one step further. I quickly realised that this was not a job for one person, and my thoughts immediately went to Julia and Chad, hoping they were up for a project where we really could work close and in-depth on this topic, which I knew had big interest and passion in the three of us. And here we are, writing our concluding thoughts on the process. In Norway, the use of digital technology has in recent years gotten increased attention as both the national curriculum opens for a much broader approach to the subject from a teacher's perspective, but also focuses more on the subject as a subject and learning and competencies in the student perspective. I believe the future is brighter than ever for the growing environment of teachers and scholars sharing our passion for digital technology in this context. The ongoing pandemic has made it ever clear that one not just must, but also should, look for solutions and approaches to support student learning in physical learning scaffolded by digital technology. The important thing to remember in this setting is that digital technology should support learning, not just being tools to measure times, steps, heart rates, and kilometres. I also believe that the student voice must not be overlooked when you want to implement these kinds of pedagogies and approaches, we are concerned about in this book. The student holds valuable insight and information on not just how digital technology is omnipresent in their everyday lives, but also how new tools and trends are emerging, and how those can be implemented in their learning environment in school. If school life can, even more, mirror the students' everyday life, it creates motivation for learning, also in a subject like PE. I hope our book creates debate, engagement, and provides support so that the topic of digital technology in PE can be embraced and further developed by a broad community of students, teachers, and researchers.

Chad

My conception and understanding of the value of FL has been so enriched and expanded through the collaborative process of writing this book with Julia and Ove! I am so grateful for the opportunity I had to work with them and learn with them/from them on this project. FL, to me, has always been an approach that teachers can leverage to help get what they want, which in the United States and many other places is mostly *time*. Teachers here do not get to see their students very often and the format of FL offers asynchronous digital space that can expand opportunities for teachers to teach and students, and possibly households, to learn and be active. Intentionally designed digital instruction can be used to promote student activity outside of the school day, engage households, and encourage community involvement, which aligns with Comprehensive School Physical Activity Program initiatives. But our goal as physical educators should not just be to leverage tools that help students accumulate a few more daily physical activity minutes. We can all agree that physical activity is important and promoting engagement outside of PE is good, but not without meaningful, deep learning happening within and alongside it. Ove and Julia helped me come to acknowledge how FL can be more than a format for promoting physical activity. It is an approach that can foster a wide range of positive outcomes across all learning domains. It is a student-centred approach with rich, embedded pedagogies that can influence deep learning, motivation, and probably more. We recognise there is much research, much practice, much reflection, and many more iterations to be developed. Indeed, we are at the beginning stages of understanding the role and value of FL in PE. After all, we included in our title 'opportunities and applications'. There are opportunities FL presents, for teachers who wish to try it and in contexts where it might provide value. The applications will vary as contexts, students, teachers, and communities vary. We encourage you to think critically about what we presented in this book. Take an iterative, reflective, and student-centred approach to embedding FL into your programs to ensure it is applied in ways that align best with your students' readiness, supports, interests, and needs.

Julia

Writing this book with Chad and Ove throughout the COVID-19 pandemic has brought my thoughts regarding the value and benefits of FL in PE to the fore. In the UK, many educators transitioned to adopting a 'blended' or 'hybrid' model of teaching when many schools were closed, and home-schooling became commonplace. This context will have challenged many of us to consider 'homework' for PE, how to better utilise online environments when teaching and learning at a distance and utilising resources we and our students had to hand to support physical activity and movement. While this learning environment may not have been our preference, and in many cases, it was a scenario in which we had little time to adapt to, it provided a steep learning curve for considering the spaces in which PE can and does take place. We may never be in such a scenario again. Yet the choice and intention to utilise the different spaces and time for learning in PE is something that FL provides us with an option in which we can add our list of tools and means to make PE 'boundaryless.'

One of the aspects that resonates to me in concluding this book is how FL can contribute to creating a learning environment that is meaningful for us and our students. We discussed aspects such as student motivation for the subject and FL's contribution towards physical activity. Yet there are many ways that PE can be meaningful for students such as through social interaction and learning that is personally relevant. FL will not be a panacea in solving 'problems' in PE or being all things to all people. But just as we tend to view technology as a tool to support us with educational processes, FL can act as a metaphorical bridge and supporting structure towards the meaningful implementation of digital technology and online learning in PE. As Fletcher and colleagues discussed in their recent book, collaboration with others both within and outside the formal boundaries of the classroom are likely to lead to a deeper awareness of what students find meaningful and they may be more likely to seek out the types of experiences in other contexts beyond PE (Fletcher et al., 2021). FL is well placed to make use of technologies that support students' experiences of meaningful learning *outside* of the classroom so this can be expanded upon *inside* the classroom. But it does not do anything on its own. We are key actors in how we engage with, apply, and develop FL.

Concluding thoughts

In authoring this book, each one of us was considering and writing about the use of FL within the context of PE. In coming together to share our critical thoughts, we have sought to provide an extensive review of how FL is being used in PE and to what ends (i.e., physical activity). This book has made significant headway in terms of considering the practical implementations of FL in PE – something that we saw extraordinarily little of up until now. The guiding principles and framework for high-quality PE that we created because of considering the theoretical and practical scene of FL in PE give us all a starting point for our practice in seeking to explore, augment, and experiment with FL. This book acts as a point of reference for those teachers, researchers, and educators in PE to harness the knowledge, ideas, and principles that we have explored and guide them in their praxis.

It is likely that due to the increasing demands of distance and online learning due to recent contexts such as COVID-19, we see more teachers trying out new or existing pedagogical practices to support their students. Similarly, it is likely that schools may begin to take a similar strategy to teaching and learning as has been seen in higher education in terms of seeking to support independent and accessible learning for students. We do not know what the future for FL and PE holds but, we believe that it is already having and will continue to have a lasting influence on the subject given its multitude of benefits.

In considering our (and others) future explorations of FL in PE, we see adopting a critical stance in terms of what technologies, strategies, and techniques allow us to extend the learning opportunities for our students. Learning what works and at what level needs to be shared for us to grow and develop our uses of approaches such as FL.

We see our students playing a vital role in developing teachers' and educators' uses of FL. Subsequently, using their ideas and empowering them to be involved in the design and use of the approach is likely to result in better outcomes for all. Furthermore, seeking to explore with students what is meaningful and where they find meaning within PE and connecting this with how we use FL we believe will be a fruitful next step. FL should have meaning for both educators and students. Yet, if we are unclear as to what is meaningful for our students then we are unlikely to be able to use FL in a way that is meaningful for them.

Reference

Fletcher, T., Ni Chroinin, D., Gleddie, G., & Beni, S. (2021). *Meaningful physical education: An approach for teaching and learning*. London: Routledge.

Index

Note: Page numbers followed by "n" refer to notes; and page numbers in **Bold** refer to tables; and page numbers in *italics* refer to figures